SHARING WISDOM, BUILDING VALUES

LETTERS FROM FAMILY BUSINESS OWNERS TO THEIR SUCCESSORS

DENISE H. KENYON-ROUVINEZ

GORDON ADLER

GUIDO CORBETTA

GIANFILIPPO CUNEO

FAMILY
ENTERPRISE
PUBLISHERS
Division of The Family Business Consulting Group, Inc.™

SHARING WISDOM, BUILDING VALUES
LETTERS FROM FAMILY BUSINESS OWNERS TO THEIR SUCCESSORS

by
Denise H. Kenyon-Rouvinez
Gordon Adler
Guido Corbetta
Gianfilippo Cuneo

Copyright ©2002, Family Enterprise Publishers™
1220-B Kennestone Circle
Marietta, Georgia 30066
800-551-0633
www.efamilybusiness.com

FIRST EDITION

To our children.

To the business families who contributed to this book.

TABLE OF CONTENTS

Those of us who work with family businesses know that our knowledge has been gleaned from the owners and leaders of the business owning families that we've had the privilege to come to know. Their experiences, insights, knowledge and sometimes good fortune have informed us concerning what works and what doesn't work for families pursuing goals together across generations.

One of the clearest lessons learned is that while every family business is unique, they also have much in common in terms of both challenges and rewards. Family firms the world over can learn mightily from one another, just as each successive generation can learn from their predecessors.

This book offers lessons from twenty-four family businesses the world over – not case studies, but the words of family business leaders themselves. Oddly, the words gain power because they are not necessarily intended for the readers of the book. Rather the words come from parents' hearts offered to their children. We fortunate readers gain intimate access to privileged family communications and lore.

The themes developed in this volume's letters touch all the essentials of family business. Subjects include the role of founders, siblings working together, the interaction of cousins, women in the family business, dealing with wealth and stewardship. Other topics deal with family business dynasties, working through difficult times, dealing with having no successors and social responsibility.

The lessons found here are universal because they come from virtually every corner of the world – Finland to Brazil, Japan to Kuwait, Italy to Singapore. The lessons are timeless because they reach so deeply into history – with Italian winemaker Marchesi Dè Frescobaldi in its 30th generation stretching back to 1092. The businesses represent industries as diverse as winemaking and appliance manufacturing. Some of the businesses have sales equivalent to just a few million dollars while others' volume is counted in billions.

The goal of each letter is the same: to share wisdom and build values so that the future can build on the past. Use this book and the letters it contains to help your family and its enterprises achieve the same.

Craig E. Aronoff, Ph.D.
Co-Founder and Principal
The Family Business Consulting Group, Inc.

THE AUTHORS

Denise Kenyon-Rouvinez, Ph.D. – Project leader

Is a Swiss-American specialist in the field of family business. In recent years she has published articles on governance issues in family businesses and on serial business families. Denise is an associate of the Family Business Consulting Group (FBCG). Founder and President of the Family Business Network (FBN) in French speaking Switzerland, she received the Family Firm Institute (FFI) Award for the 2001 best doctoral dissertation as well as the "Prof. Emeritus Alden G. Lank Award" for best paper in October 2000 in London. She worked for four years at IMD, among other doing research on family businesses.

Gordon Adler

Is an American writer, management communications expert and writing coach. Since 1996, he has been Senior Writer at IMD, where he has worked closely with FBN and family business faculty. He works as an editor/writing/communications consultant at leading management institutions and international firms. He has published in a number of leading journals and magazines.

Guido Corbetta

Is a professor of strategic management. He is also the founder of family business programs and chairman of the strategic and entrepreneurial management department of Bocconi University School of Management, Milan, Italy. Guido Corbetta is also a member of the Family Business Consulting Group International. He has authored many books and articles on family business issues.

Gianfilippo Cuneo

Is the founder of Bain & Co, Italy, and of the venture capital fund: Angelventures. Until 1989 he was a Director of McKinsey. Mr. Cuneo is well known in Italy for his top management consulting activities for major Italian corporations. He has written four books on management and numerous articles for the leading Italian business newspapers.

INTRODUCTION

A 1998 survey[1] of 3,200 company successions in France between 1986 and 1997 revealed that nearly 30% of the companies failed in the seven years after the transition. Start-ups, notorious for fragility, fail only half as often. Of all the difficulties family businesses face, succession is one of the most important, and one of the most challenging. Why is it so difficult to get succession right?

One of the challenges of succession, for many a family business, is that three kinds of leadership rest on the shoulders of one person, or perhaps on a small team. Succession is therefore, not merely succession of management, as it would most likely be in a publicly-held company, but also succession of ownership and succession of family leadership – perhaps all at the same time. When the outgoing leader has held the position for a long time, major, complex, unsettling upheaval can result, for the family and the business. Here is how Mariano Puig of the Puig Corporation, Spain, describes the succession problem: "Unlike multinationals that change CEOs every five years, and which are well accustomed to the process, for Puig Corp., it was a difficult process: we had only ever been exposed to one transition in our history, and it had happened 45 years ago!"[2]

Sharing Wisdom, Building Values was borne of our conviction that succession matters and long-surviving family businesses can teach us valuable lessons. Imagine having the opportunity to ask the leaders of successful family businesses from around the world what stories and lessons they would pass on to the next generations. That is the purpose of this book – to give members of successful family companies a "podium" from which to share their tales, values, principles, and secrets. *Sharing Wisdom, Building Values* offers you the words of leaders of large and small businesses from various industry sectors; large and small families; first generation to thirty-first generation family businesses from different continents and a variety of cultures and religions. There are letters from the past and letters or testimonies for future generations on business, family, values – and, of course, succession. There are rich descriptions of how founders, siblings or cousins cope with succession, how women play an impor-

v

tant role in family businesses, how family dynasties have survived through many centuries and how values and stewardship of capital can be passed to the next generation. Topical themes are covered too: shared leadership, generational skip, how some families cope with difficult times, and how one generation can inculcate a sense of social responsibility in the next generation. The letters have been grouped in chapters by one particularly important theme they portray; however, most cover several topics and are worth considering from different perspectives.

The letters in *Sharing Wisdom, Building Values* highlight the truth that there is no unique formula for family business success. One family accepts all family members and in-laws into the business; another restricts entry and curbs family involvement. One family dislikes the idea of floating the business; another embraces it. One family wins on specializing; another banks on diversification. No matter what values and principles a family business stands for, and the choices it makes to succeed, the letters in this book highlight at least one overarching lesson: each family, regardless of size, country, culture, and religion, can reconcile the best practices from other businesses, from theory, from their own business and family contexts, and from the cultures in which they live and work, to manage fruitfully their own family businesses over generations. Herein lies the magic of this collection: each family has found a way to incorporate its own culture and values into its business strategy for the benefit of both the family and the business. The resulting richness and diversity is one of the many beauties of family businesses.

This book came to fruition with a great deal of invaluable and often unsung help. First and foremost, we are indebted to each and every family in the book for the time they gave and the effort they made, their commitment to the project, their sincerity and generosity. We are deeply grateful for their sharing not only successful moments, but also their periods of doubt and business trouble, and, when they did, for not glossing over the difficult issues. Taken together, these rich, varied and often intensely personal testimonies offer an enduring message of hope to families in business.

We would also like to express our gratitude to MM. Lombard Odier & Cie for sponsoring this project. Their sponsorship went beyond mere support – more than a dozen special people gave freely and tirelessly of their time and expertise. Special thanks go also to Gianfilippo Cuneo and Guido Corbetta for inspiring us with their book on Italian family businesses, Lettere al futuro – Il passaggio dell'azienda da una generazione all'atra. Le testimonianze di 33 imprenditori di successo, and for allowing us to reprint two of their letters.

[1]Banque du développement des PME, Fall 1998 – cited in Le Nouvel Economiste No. 1114, October 30, 1998.

[2]Family Business Network Conference, Paris, France, October 1998.

A number of other people have helped us bring this book to completion by providing links and contacts to families around the world. We would like, in particular, to thank members of the Family Business Network: Jose G. Villarreal C., Peter May, Sonia Totten and Joachim Schwass; members of The Family Business Consulting Group International: Tamar Milo, Amy Schuman and Nancy Waichler; as well as Cynthia Georgeson from S.C. Johnson, Angele Vermeersch from the Mulliez Family Office, Francisco Valera from Valera & Associates in Spain, Jorge A. Castillo from Consultores de Empresas Familiares in Mexico, and Gillian Kang in Singapore. All provided a wonderful example of cooperation between countries. We also want to give a special thank you to Professors Craig Aronoff and John Ward, who believed in this project and gave us the motivation to carry it through.

Thierry Lombard, Senior Partner of the Lombard Odier Darier Hentsch & Cie Bank, conveys his personal reflections on the philosophy, the history and the future of this company, which is presently in the hands of the 6th generation of the Lombard and Odier families.

Geneva, June 19, 2002

The recent events involving our bank – Lombard Odier & Co. – have made me think a lot and now prompt me to commit to writing some personal reflections on our history and on my hopes for our bank's future.

Our bank is a general partnership, completely in private hands. The managing partners are jointly liable for the bank's commitments to the full extent of their personal assets. Our bank's statutes provide for no specific rights concerning **succession**. The future of our company depends mainly on the qualities and the personalities of those who manage it, so selecting future partners is, by consequence, of paramount importance.

Indeed, the nomination of a new managing partner can only be made by a unanimous vote of the current managing partners, and it must be motivated by the company's interest in gaining complementary competencies, personality and integrity. The children of partners, even if they enter the bank's employ, have no guarantee of becoming a partner. It is true that they bring a special family and cultural background, but they can climb the career ladder only on the strength of their competence and their personality. These are not written rules, but rather a form of culture handed down from generation to generation.

Letter from Alexis E. Lombard (3rd generation) to his son Albert

Aix, April 28, 1898

My Dear Son,

…Be well aware that these studies are a gift and a privilege that many young people would like to have and that in today's business world **one must** be educated and even well-educated…

Letter from Alexis E. Lombard (3rd generation) to his son Albert

Geneva, October 10, 1903

My Dear Son,

…The visits that I have made, and the people I have seen and talked with in the city prove to me more and more that we have to keep ourselves up to date with what is going on. The Swiss banks, among others, are extremely active, sending their managers to gather information and we must not let ourselves be overtaken by them. For you, in particular, and the position you will hold in the company, it is essential that you bring your share of knowledge in this field. Gustave Hentsch has worked hard and taken notes; you no doubt will do the same in your turn. Your time will be well taken up between the office, correspondence and your social duties, but you must put your back into it...

Letter from Alexis E. Lombard (3rd generation) to his son Albert

Geneva, February 22, 1904

My Dear Son,

...I am talking to you very frankly because you know the importance we attach to your undergoing a full training in the United States. In the middle of the chaos which rules everywhere in Europe, it is still to the United States that one turns willingly, not at all because the country is perfect, but because it is still the one, along with England, where there is the most financial morality...

The history of a company and the destiny of the people who work in it are sometimes surprising. Recently we have taken a strategic decision that will have no small impact on the future of private banking in Geneva. On 3 June, a little more than two weeks ago, we publicly announced our decision to merge – I prefer the phrase "to associate ourselves" – with Geneva's oldest private bank, Messrs. Darier Hentsch & Co. This is a natural **association,** because on the one hand we enjoy very strong and longstanding links, and on the other hand we share common values and a history that have been the key basis of our mutual capacity for harmonious rapprochement.

It is to our greatest pleasure that we therefore find ourselves being a company managed by fourteen partners, a collection of personalities, experiences, talents and horizons.

Messrs. Lombard Odier & Co. - Brief History

1798   The Henri Hentsch & Lombard bank was founded by Messrs. Jean-Gédéon Lombard and Henri Hentsch

1830   Charles Odier joined the bank

1852   Founding member of the Geneva Stock Exchange

1905   Founding member of the Swiss National Bank

1919   Creation of an employee retirement fund, one of the first pension plans in Switzerland

1957   Pioneer in banking computing

1979   First European bank to acquire a seat on the NYSE

2002   Merger with Messrs. Darier Hentsch & Co.

Destiny has done it again: my ancestor, Jean-Gédéon Lombard, began as a clerk at Henri Hentsch, with whom he became an partner on June 19, 1798. Two-hundred and four years later, almost to the day, we announce the merger of our two companies.

Messrs. Darier Hentsch & Co. - Brief History

1796   The Hy Hentsch & Co. bank was founded

1798   The Henri Hentsch & Lombard bank was founded by Messrs. Jean-Gédéon Lombard and Henri Hentsch

1830   Forerunner of companies in the "business of welcoming foreigners"

1880   Took an active part in financing the Swiss railway network, then in creating insurance companies and savings banks

1991   Merger between Messrs. Darier & Co. and Messrs. Hentsch & Co.

2002   Merger with Messrs. Lombard Odier & Co.

Over the past 200 years, the history and development of Messrs. Lombard Odier & Co. and Messrs. Darier Hentsch & Co. have been tempered by the personalities of their managing partners. With the passing of the generations, we have had men capable of taking major strategic decisions and difficult gambles. They were able to emerge from their Swiss cocoon and anticipate, in particular, the need for internationalisation.

At the outset, the college of partners comprised only founding family members, but then it extended itself progressively, first to the 'family' (in the broad sense) and finally to include outside personalities. This progression clearly denotes our desire to be open to the world and to different ideas:

1796
Hy Hentsch & Co.

1798
Henri Hentsch & Lombard
Henri Hentsch, Jean-Gédéon Lombard

1800-1815
J. G. Lombard et J. J. Lullin

1809-1991
Hentsch & Co.

1816-1825
Jean Gédéon Lombard & Co.

1880-1991
Darier & Co.

1826-1830
Lombard, Bonna & Co.

1991-2002
Darier Hentsch & Co.

1830-2002
Lombard Odier & Co.

2002
Lombard Odier Darier Hentsch & Co.
Pierre Darier, Thierry Lombard, Thierry Kern, Bertrand Darier, Jean Bonna,
Eric Demole, Patrick Odier, Richard de Tscharner, Jacques Rossier, Philippe Sarasin,
Jean Pastré, Barthélemy Helg, Bernard Droux, Anne-Marie de Weck

All through our history, we can trace three constant **characteristics** that have contributed to our success and that will, I believe, still contribute to it in the future:

1. Audacity, but with caution!
It was not only his sense of adventure that was beckoning Alexandre Lombard when he headed passionately towards America in the 1840s. It was also the need to turn towards new markets, in view of the instability pervading Europe, and the increasing mistrust that he felt towards the security of European funds. Here was the audacity of being among the first to be interested in the New World, along with caution in the form of in-depth financial studies he undertook to determine the reliability of potential investments.

The Diary of Alexandre Etienne Lombard

September 20, 1847

The commercial outlook is bleak indeed, with one disaster following another. The London market has been rocked by huge bankruptcies. One cannot predict the extent of the repercussions. This crisis has been foreseen for a long time and it has at last arrived with great intensity. I don't know if we shall be able to escape its impact! I am hopeful that we can, due to the reserve we have adopted for a long time and especially in recent months. However, the general depreciation in values is hitting us from another direction, through some shares that we failed to get rid of in time. We are lucky though to have sold the greater part of them. Thus we are in the clear and can ride events without too many concerns. What is painful is to see all around the bleeding wounds inflicted by the disaster upon the financial values of some fortunes; and yet what we can see from our contacts and customers is very little, because our operations were limited to a great extent to our customers' means, and if they are losing at all, they can absorb their losses easily.

It is at times like these that one appreciates the advantages of having acted with moderation. I only wish we had acted even more cautiously for everybody's sake.

2. Economic rationality and ethics.

Since our beginnings, members of our family have been keen to temper the financial and economic interests of the bank with a profound ethical awareness. Even back in 1840, Alexandre Lombard had as a criterion for investment in any of the states in the United States the presence or otherwise of slavery. He was firmly convinced that there can be no durable development without a healthy basis. For him, it went without saying that a society founded upon an immoral principle was doomed to ruination sooner or later.

3. Adaptability.

Throughout its six generations of history, our bank and above all the men who have made it what it is today have understood how to adapt to all situations and to the evolution of our society. In 1898, the bank numbered sixteen employees; today it employs over 1,500 and it will soon employ 2,000. For us, adaptability means a change in the continuity, with respect to our values and our traditions.

Letter from Alexis E. Lombard (3rd generation) to his son Albert

Aix, August 7, 1899

My Dear Son,

...since I have been in business, it is true there has been a considerable transformation; at the beginning, the Bank, or more strictly speaking, exchange and gold transactions, occupied an important place in education and in commercial activities. Today, the railways, telegraph and telephone have changed everything, rapid communications open new worlds, electricity is transforming the world, and it is naturally up to the Bank to supply the capital for all of these changes. In order to do this intelligently, one has to know something about it...

In our links with Geneva and its history, we also have a long, robust tradition of social, cultural and humanitarian responsibility.

At the level of the bank and our way of managing the business, there are also **principles of management** that have been and will continue to be our strength:

1. The balance between financial science and human psychology.
We have always sought a fair combination of the two. Those who have mastered the technical aspects do not have priority over those who understand the world and its psychology.

2. Structure.
We have always favoured a small, prudent and focused structure. It seems essential to me that every owner of our bank must also be one of its managers. Living in the company helps to understand it and to remain in permanent contact with the client. Floating the company would mean a loss of contact; it would completely change our way of doing business and our whole corporate culture. A former colleague used to say this to me: 'At Lombard Odier, one loves one's colleagues and one cherishes one's clients'. This is an integral part of our culture.

3. A willingness to listen and intense collaboration among specialists.
As partners, whilst still mastering our trade, we owe it to ourselves to remain generalists, ever ready to listen to the client to understand him and interpret his needs. We share with each client much more than the technical side of the stock market. We take into account his relations, his family, his contacts, and the future of his professional and private wealth. We have a long-term responsibility towards our clients.

4. Remaining anti-cyclical.
We do our best not to follow the fashion. We try to keep in mind the tremendous opportunity provided by our private structure, namely not to favour the short-term to the detriment of the long-term. Not following the fashion enables us to see possibilities that others don't wish to see or are unable to see or exploit, while on the other hand, it allows us to be present in markets that can appear not to be profitable in the short-term.

5. Re-engineering.
We rethink our action plans calmly, creating tomorrow's company based on a respect for the past and for tradition.

6. Responsibility.
We work to develop a feeling of security for our activities, which enables us to devote our total energy to the quality of services and products we offer the client.

In order to ensure continuity in our business, we have always been deeply attached to our fundamental **values:** ethics, confidentiality, excellence and responsibility. This responsibility manifests itself with respect to three elements: the employees and their families, the customers and the company. We are totally responsible for continuing to manage our company through thick and thin, and cannot hide ourselves in anonymity.

Our ambitious objectives have always made us quick in decision making and capable of seizing opportunities or occasions. Of course, growing from eight to fourteen partners within Lombard Odier Darier Hentsch may be seen as a brake. However, it can also be a help: an important decision will only be taken when there is a general consensus, and so there is an accumulation of prudence and wisdom guiding the business. By the day the decision is taken, the level of decision maturity and analysis has increased significantly. All through our history, the fact of not having only one captain on board has prevented many errors.

Letter from Alexis E. Lombard (3rd generation) to his son Albert

Geneva, October 2, 1898

My Dear Son,

...Never have we seen more clearly that work is a blessing and that we must learn early on to look after others – whether this be for the nation for those who can – or any other useful project; for this, you must build relationships among all the classes and not stay within a narrow circle...I urge you to think carefully and not to allow yourself to be stopped by remarks from any friends with more limited horizons...

A very strong aspect of **our future** is the contribution of our customers in an opening onto the world and its evolution. Through them we have an important and powerful source of information. This is a great wealth. Our customers push us to strive for excellence and innovation. It is very important for us to be able to, and to know how to look after clients from generation to generation.

The best way of ensuring the future of our company is to keep it in gòod health: competitive, motivating and profitable. For a private company this is the only long-term guarantee. The continuity of our company depends on people who share the same passion, motivation and ethics. We shall continue building build it, and have the ambition of handing it down to a 7th and even an 8th generation.

Finally, if I should conclude with a message for our next generation of partners, I would say this: Our bank is a private company taking care each day to forge its future with respect for the past, accepting the present and wishing to adapt itself to the future and to harmonize these three time spans. We expect of you that:

1. You be capable of respecting the past and of being different;

2. You realise that every decision taken today will have its impact tomorrow. In fact, certain decisions that can be justified in the short-term lose their justification and can have negative or destructive effects in the long-term.

Thank you for your differences, thank you for your enthusiasm, and bravo for your competencies and your technological expertise. Never hesitate to delve into our history to find the rules and the principles that will equip you to be different and better in the exercise of your profession as private banker, which can be practised only with passion and modesty.

Thierry Lombard

Succession Tips and Tools

Although family businesses may differ significantly from one to the next, our work with numerous families suggests that the following thoughts may ease the succession process:

1. Planning

Planning for succession well ahead of time can be a vital element of success in transmitting the business to the next generation. Succession planning can easily span five to ten years, for it includes, among other tasks, strategic planning, estate planning and sound tax planning that will leave the family and the business with a manageable tax burden at the time of the effective handover. As Léon Danco said, "It is never too early to start planning for succession."[3]

2. Identifying, training and empowering successors

Identifying successors may not be easy. Parents may wonder: Will the children be good leaders for our business? How can we decide which of the children is the best successor? Parents may grapple with conflicting imperatives here: they wish to serve the best interests of the business, while, at the same time, they also wish to be good parents and preserve family harmony. In such decisions, the company board or external advisors may provide neutral, fair and respected judgment. Once identified, successors may need to be trained and empowered. One family business owner told us, "The best way to train successors is to trust them, and accept that making mistakes is part of the learning process."

3. Separating business, family and ownership issues

Since family members are often involved as managers, shareholders and family members, separating business, family and ownership issues may be a difficult challenge in a family business environment. During succession, however, it may be advantageous to delineate the business, the family and the ownership clearly. In the business, the family faces succession both in management and on the board. It is possible – though not easy – to manage succession on both these levels at the same time, but often, succession in management comes first, since the retiring generation usually keeps a board position before retiring completely. Family plays an important role in succession and in the future success of the family business since it is the foundation of the family beliefs and values that play a key role in the perennity of the family business. It may be valuable to separate ownership issues from family and business issues, and for owners to keep in mind that, while being an owner may grant rights, it also implies duties and commitment. Over the past few years, emphasis on the role and importance of owners has increased.

4. Managing conflicts

When it comes to conflict, compared with other businesses, family businesses are often at a disadvantage. The overlap between family, management and ownership can make interactions between family members difficult at times. During periods of succession, when uncertainty is high, conflicts may increase in depth and in frequency. To prepare for conflicts and minimize their impact, it may help to be aware of three pieces of advice:

- Conflict is inevitable. It happens in almost every business and almost every family. Put two people together and, at some stage, their differences are likely to clash – they have different roles, needs, goals and perspectives.

- The longer a conflict simmers or remains repressed, the harder it may be for the parties involved to resolve it amicably.

- There is a positive side to conflicts: they can help in revisiting issues and bolster creativity. You can make them work for you and for your business.

5. A sound governance structure

The form of governance structure depends on the stage at which the family and the business find themselves. It also depends on the size of the family and the degree to which family members are involved in ownership and in the business. A good business board, with independent external directors, can often provide good guidance for the business and help with succession. If the family is large and only some members are active in the business, a family council can help deal with such family matters as education, family holidays, family investments and the family's involvement in society at large. When the business has a large number of family shareholders, or when the family is more involved as owners than as managers of the business, a shareholders' board may offer advantages.

6. A family constitution

Consider writing a family constitution or protocol. Clarify the family's vision and mission for the business. Set clear rules and goals for family members. Doing all this can ease the typical problems of succession. Going through the process of writing a family constitution can take a long time, but it also fortifies the bonds among family members. By sketching guidelines and values, family members may gain a more profound understanding of their family values, what they as a family want for the business, and why they are in business together. Going through a family constitution often gives family members a sense of responsibility, pride and belonging. It can foster family unity and commitment. Experience has taught us that while lawyers and consultants can help by providing guidelines and support throughout the process, they should not write the document for you. Why? Because going through the process of discussing the various issues and preparing the document is at least as important as the document itself.

7. Communication

Whatever your plans may be, communicate them. Owners, family, employees, customers and suppliers have a right and a need to know what is likely to happen with the business. All too often, excellent potential successors leave the family business because they have not been told that there is a future in the business for them. All too often, older-generation leaders stay on because no members of the younger generation have expressed a desire to be successors. Try to make successors feel wanted in the business. Make them feel proud of their family and its commitment to the business. Work to help the retiring generation and other family members learn to trust the successors. Good communication can help family members iron out their conflicts and express their love.

Sharing Wisdom, Building Values is a book you can keep referring to for years to come, for real-life examples never lose their value, and it is our hope that this book will touch you and give you ideas for preparing your business and your family for succession.

[3]Family Business Network Conference, Paris, France, October 1998.

I

FOUNDERS

Founders of family dynasties and family businesses are a special breed. Often, as various examples in this book show, they are visionary people with strong characters. They seem to have a need to succeed both in launching their businesses and in making them different from others. Henry Ford had a vision: everyone should be able to afford a car. At the time, his foresight seemed odd, but ultimately, he turned out to be right. Ruben Rausing, the founder of Tetra Pak, and Walt Disney had both a vision – create a whole new market where none existed before – and the determination to develop it.

Marcel Bich did not invent the ballpoint pen, nor did he like using ballpoints: the ink ran, they were messy, and everyone who had tried to produce a better quality had failed. But when an order came in, Marcel Bich decided that if he was going to supply ballpoint pens, he was going to supply top quality. He spared no effort. To support top-of-the range research, he invested more money than his small company was making at the time. For three years he searched for the finest machinery and the best technicians. But no one believed in his venture. No bank supported his efforts. And yet his stubbornness paid off: after three years of effort, he had a well-functioning, non-messy ballpoint pen in his hand. His vision was simple: to produce high-quality, low-cost ballpoint pens that everyone could afford. Not stopping with pens, he later applied his low-cost, high-quality rule to razors and lighters. Today everyone either owns or has owned at least one Bic product.

Founders of successful family businesses often have strong values that they instill in the next generation. These same values, in many cases, are still very much in evidence a few generations down the line. A good illustration is

1

the letter from the Murugappa family later in this book. However, once they have created a business and instilled strong values, founders often struggle to let go. In our work and research we have encountered many family businesses that failed because the patriarch refused to hand over the leadership of the business to the next generation.

Strong values and the difficulty of letting go are evident in the family business founders in this chapter. Fritz Henkel, Abdurrahman Paksoy and Marcel Bich – all are men of strong character and deep-seated principles. Fritz Henkel handed his business over in 1929 and died in 1930; Marcel Bich organized his whole succession, handed over the business and passed away the night before the first annual general meeting at which he was not to preside. Letting go of the business may not have been easy for them, but the perennity of the business was paramount for both. Each took considerable time to think about succession. Both put good structures and competent successors in place. They knew their own children were competent business leaders. They knew their children shared the family values because they had been working hand-in-hand for a very long time – thirty years in the Henkel case and almost forty years in the case of the Bich family.

By contrast, the letter from Enric Bernat of Chupa Chups – the man behind Kojak's world-famous lollipop (from the popular American television series *Kojak*) – gives us the rare example of a founder who not only let go of the business and found a life after, but who also praises his children for taking the decision to withdraw from executive management.

Henkel KGaA

Location: Düsseldorf, Germany

Turnover (in US$): $ 11.447 billion (2001)

Date of exchange rate: March 25, 2002

Name of local currency: Euro

Number of employees: 45,753 (Dec 31, 2001)

Activity/industry sector:
Consumer brands and technologies: Laundry and home care (23% of total sales, including brands such as Persil, Mir, etc.); cosmetics/toiletries (16% of total sales, including brands such as Schwarzkopf, Fa, Diadermin, etc.); adhesives for consumers and craftsmen (10% of total sales, including brands such as Pritt, Pattex, etc.); Henkel Technologies (22% of total sales); Corporate, Cognis, Henkel-Ecolab (29% of total sales).

Geographic spread of the business (2001, % of total sales):
Germany (23%); rest of Europe, Middle-East and Africa (49%); North America (15%); Latin America (5%); Asia Pacific (8%).

Year the business was started: 1876

Name of the founder and relation to the author: Fritz Henkel (1848 – 1930)

Generation running the business:
Members of the 4th and 5th generation are Chairmen and members of the Supervisory Board and Shareholders' Committee of Henkel KGaA.

Name & position of person writing the letters (1899, 1929):
Fritz Henkel, founder, owner and general manager of the company.

% of capital owned by the family:
56.87% of the voting rights in KGaA are held by 62 members of the families of the descendants of Fritz Henkel, the company's founder, and by companies and foundations appointed by those families.

Recipient(s) of the letter: Fritz Henkel Jr., son of the founder.

Actual letters sent from Fritz Henkel Sr.
to Fritz Henkel Jr.

Fritz Henkel Sr., 1876   *Fritz Henkel Jr., 1893*

Fritz Henkel

Düsseldorf, December 22, 1899

My Dear Fritz,

With this letter I confer in you the power of attorney in our company, and I have no doubt in my mind that it will fill you with pride just as it fills me with pride to hand it over to you. You know, my dear son, that your duties are many and your responsibility is almost as great as mine. You are now called to work at expanding our business and removing part of my job from my tired shoulders.

I feel sincerely happy and relieved to have found a devoted employee in you.

With all my love,

Your father

HENKEL & CIE. G.M.B.H.   DÜSSELDORF

KOMMERZIENRAT FRITZ HENKEL

Regensdorf, July 25, 1929

My Dear Son Fritz,

You are celebrating your birthday today. Congratulations!

Twenty-five years ago, I took you in as a partner in my business. We have, since then, worked cheerfully and seriously together, and I would like to thank you with all my heart for your faithful collaboration. Today, the Henkel company is one of the largest and one of the healthiest businesses in Germany, and it is highly esteemed, not only in Germany, but also abroad. My dear son Fritz, we want to continue to do our duty together and work happily for the future well being of our company.

With all my love,

Your father

Société BIC

Location: Clichy, France

Turnover (in US$): $1376 million (2001)

Date of exchange rate: April 25, 2002

Name of local currency: Euros

Number of employees: 9,700

Activity/industry sector (net sales by products):
Stationery (52%); lighters (25%); shavers (20%); others (3%).

Geographic spread of the business:
Western Europe (30%); North & Central America (54%); Latin America (8%); rest of the world (8%).

Year the business was started: 1945

Name of the founder and relation to the author: Baron Marcel Bich, author.

Generation running the business: 2nd

Name & position of person writing the letter: Baron Marcel Bich, then President & CEO.

Family members active in the business:
Bruno BICH, Chief Executive Officer; François BICH, Executive Vice President and Category Manager Lighters; Marie-Aimée BICH DUFOUR, Executive Vice President and General Counsel.

% of capital owned by the family as of December 31, 2000: 34% (49.5% voting rights).

Recipient(s) of the letter: All shareholders of Société BIC in 1973.

Short history:
In 1945, Marcel Bich acquired, with his friend, Edouard Buffard, a small company that produced components for fountain pens in Clichy, France. In 1950, after two years of research and efforts to produce a good quality and reliable item, he launched his first ballpoint pen, which he called "BIC," a shortened, easy-to-remember version of his own name. He spent the next 20 years refining the technology behind what seems to be a simple product but, in fact, requires technology and precision to produce. Following his motto "provide consumers around the world with quality products at affordable prices," he introduced BIC® lighters (1973) and later BIC® shavers (1975). Now, every day, Société BIC sells more that 21 million stationery products, 4 million lighters and 9 million shavers.

Source: Bich L. (2001). *Le Baron Bich. Un homme de pointe.* France: Editions Perrin.

The Bich family in Newport, 1970

Letter from Marcel BICH to the shareholders

Annual Meeting, June 4th, 1973

Dear Shareholders,

We are assembling for the first time since the Initial Public Offering of our company shares on the Paris Stock Exchange on November 15, 1972. I would like to take this opportunity to tell you how I perceive the principles underlying the conduct of our business.

These principles have been developed over the last twenty years, since I founded and have since run the Company. They were not shaped by a formal education from a French or American business school, but rather by the tough school of hands-on business that I entered at the age of 18 through the smallest door. There is no denying that I deserve to be called a moneymaker: our company was started in 1953 with an initial investment of 10,000 francs and has grown today to 150 million francs par-value share capital through internally generated funds. Equity has nearly doubled each year over the last 20 years.

One of the bases of this development is the ability to take chances. Potential gains increase in proportion to risks taken. The more you risk the bigger your chances of winning...or losing. The most practical solution is to cover all risk from the start, and then you can't lose. This explains why you will not find in our balance sheet any medium- or long-term debt, a rare occurrence in today's world, where currency devaluation makes borrowing very tempting.

The second principle on which our business is founded involves fostering our staff's sense of responsibility. Our company is all but technocratic. We believe, for example, that one does not keep a rein on the price of beef by controlling retail prices, but rather by raising beef cattle. Technocracy is the evil of our times; starting at the top (many French leaders are graduates of the top Public Administration School in the country – E.N.A.), it spreads to all levels. Technocracy is particularly appealing to French people, who tend to be analytical in the Cartesian sense. It produces a crowd of administrators and organizers, but when it comes to doing the actual work, there is no one around to roll up their sleeves.

Technocracy results in a high production cost and, more alarming, low morale among employees who become bored with jobs in which they can't take any initiative. By placing confidence in workers, employees and executives, everything becomes easier. Contrary to popular belief, free and independent businesses today have a greater shot at success than ever before. As proof, just look at the increasingly serious problems with which large state-owned companies are struggling.

Furthermore, in order for a business to truly prosper, it must operate on a worldwide scale. This requires financial, industrial and commercial strength. This necessary strength, and equally essential reliance on individuals, are diametrically opposite notions. Here lies a fundamental contradiction that is difficult to solve. BIC tries to rise to the challenge in its day-to-day practice: "necessity is the mother of invention."

Yours faithfully,

Marcel BICH

Chairman & Chief Executive Officer
SOCIÉTÉ BIC

Paksoy Tic San A.S.

Location: Adana, Turkey

Turnover (in US$): $50 million

Date of exchange rate: January 1, 2002

Name of local currency: Turkish Lira

Number of employees: 250

Activity/industry sector: Food manufacturing

Geographic spread of the business: Nationwide and Middle East

Year the business was started: 1951

Name of the founder and relation to the author: Abdurrahman B. Paksoy, grandfather

Generation running the business: 3rd

Name & position of person writing the letter (1951): Abdurrahman B. Paksoy, founder

Family members active in the business: Ibrahim Paksoy, CEO; Ugur Paksoy, Chairman

Other family members non-active shareholders: About 20

% of capital owned by the family: 92%

Recipient(s) of the letter: Second generation members of the Paksoy family

Note:
Abdurrahman B. Paksoy, the founder of the business, had seven sons. Five were educated abroad, four in Europe (France and England) and one in the USA. All five were trained as engineers; most were civil engineers. After their return to Turkey, they started working as contractors on big projects.

The Abdurrahman family had been in Adana for 250 years. They were from a farming background (cotton). In 1950, Abdurrahman decided that he would get all his sons together and start a cotton ginning company. The company started operating in 1951. When Abdurrahman passed away in 1953, his sons took over. Initially, five brothers were involved in the company. The two remaining brothers were active in the agricultural side of the business. All were shareholders. Not equal shareholders, but shareholders nonetheless.

In 1954, the Paksoy family set up a plant to crush cotton oil from cotton seeds.

An oil business was started and it grew rapidly. In 1960, a soap manufacturing facility was added, and in 1974, after the 3rd generation entered the business, a margarine plant was started. Today Paksoy produces margarine, oil and soap. The gin was shut down in 1956 and sold. The family is no longer in the original business.

Today, only two of the brothers are alive, and none of them is active in the business. Two cousins of the third generation – Ibrahim and Ugur – are running it.

No members of the 4th generation are involved in the business yet. It may be difficult to involve them in the business since the young ones all want to go to Istanbul. Adana is a big city, with about 1.5 million inhabitants, but Istanbul has more to offer and is attracting all the talents. However, one member of the 4th generation is showing an interest.

The third generation still lives up to the standards set up by their grandfather. At least in as much as modern life makes it possible. Unfortunately, since 1950 society has changed dramatically. In most cases, it is very difficult to resolve differences amicably, and courts and judges have to be used more often than the family would like to. The family tries to live in the spirit of the letter more than to its precise words; family members try to instil their grandfather's precepts to their own children.

Abdurrahman Bagdadizade Paksoy to his sons

January 24, 1951

Advice for my sons,

To live in tranquillity and happily and to be successful, remember:

1. Be just, sincere and serious in all your deeds and speech. When in doubt, choose the lesser of evils and clear your conscience.

2. Always obey the rules of conscience and law.

3. Act with determination and avoid being doubtful.

4. Feel free. Do not be helpless, lazy or shy.

5. Do not be fearful of any danger. Try to be cautious, defend yourself, drive away danger. Do not fear humiliation. Often, fear itself does more damage than the danger you are trying to avoid.

6. Try to get to know as many people as possible and make more friends. In your relations, let seriousness and sincerity rule. People will thus be satisfied. Never resort to flattery or hypocrisy.

7. If you expect friendliness, you should behave sincerely, for sincerity is the only way to be received with real friendliness.

8. Select your words carefully. Spoken words may have positive or negative effects depending on the manner and timing of your speech. A man's worth and value is measured by his words.

9. Never have the all-knowing attitude. Never brag to or argue with friends. Never criticize anybody. No matter who the other person is, always assume that he is more knowledgeable, more valuable and a better person than you are.

10. In trials and auctions, always take a positive approach. Never neglect to pursue your rights through the law.

11. Never submit to your feelings, always control yourself and never get angry or violent.

12. Never talk about the evil deeds of others. Do not blame people or speak badly in their absence because such acts will lead to offence and hurt.

13. Do not mistreat people who have wronged you, even when you are capable of doing so. Always forgive. In such cases, your forgiveness is very meaningful. Sometimes wrong deeds are merely faults, careless acts or the results of misunderstandings. Even with friends and siblings, settling an argument can be painful and may cause ungrounded animosity. It is best

to act with care and prudence, as if nothing has happened. Nobody will mistreat good people; they will wrong people only if they consider them evil. Do not let anybody mistake you as an evil person; avoid creating such an image.

14. Never envy anybody; try to surpass them.

15. Do not ever promise anybody anything. Remember: a promise has to be fulfilled under all circumstances.

16. On occasions like religious holidays, never neglect visits – they are human debts.

17. Be a good citizen. Participate in elections. It is your duty to your country.

18. Be content. Contentment is not laziness; on the contrary, it is being satisfied with your life. Work as if you will never die. People who are contented will be happy; there will be no happiness otherwise.

19. Remember: it is impossible to be successful in every venture. Do not be discouraged if you fail. Believe in destiny and luck. Be a believer. Have faith. These will help you in case of loss and accidents, for you will grieve less.

20. Keep your conscience clear always.

To do others good, remember:

1. Do others favours and help them as much as you can regardless of who they are. Helping will not always be possible, but always try to find opportunities to help others. Thank them rather than expecting their thanks. Do these deeds for their own sake; expect nothing in return. Your reward is the happiness they have given you. Be extra careful not to hurt another person's pride or feelings. This is very important, for otherwise, you would be giving a spoonful and taking it back with the spoon's handle.

2. Be unselfish. Unselfishness is a virtue. Goodness is being a good person and doing good for others. Doing good can assume many faces, even showing somebody the right way to jump into water to save somebody's life. Your good deeds will vary, from the ones you do for your son, your brother, your parents, neighbours, friends, to the ones you do ones you do for people you do not like, even your enemies. But all are good deeds. Their value differs, but those who receive them will have happiness accordingly.

As for financial matters, keep in mind:

1. Material matters reveal people's ethics. Be very honest and correct in your accounts so that no disputes will arise – whether siblings or other parties

are involved. Carelessness always causes disorder and irregularity in financial matters, and the effects will be worse if the disorder and irregularity is among the siblings or if their wives are also involved.

2. Parents should treat their children impartially. Any inequality could easily lead to conflict among the children. Considering this: I tried to achieve equality by keeping a separate account for each of you. I advise you do the same for your children.

3. If conflicts arise, whatever the reasons, name three to five arbitrators and abide by their judgement, no matter what.

Above all, remember: it is easy to snap one yarn, but ten together are not easy to break. My sons, God willing, you will be happy and successful all your lives.

Your father

Chupa Chups Group

(Chupa Chups S.A. - the parent company and subsidiaries)

Headquarters Location: Barcelona, Spain

Turnover (in US$): $381.8 million (2001)

Date of exchange rate: May 27, 2002

Name of local currency: Euro

Number of employees: 2,000

Activity/industry sector: Confectionery brands: Chupa Chups, Smint, Crazy Planet.

Geographic spread of the business: Sales in 170 countries, 91% of turnover outside Spain.

Year the business was started: 1958

Name of the founder: Enric Bernat Fontlladosa

Generation running the business: 2nd

Name & position of person writing the letter: Enric Bernat, founder

Other family members in the business through the Board of Directors: Xavier Bernat Serra, President; Ramon Bernat Serra, Vice-President; Marcos Bernat Serra, Vice-President; Marta Bernat Serra; Nina Bernat Serra; Nuria Serra Roig.

% of capital owned by the family: 100%

Recipient(s) of the letter: Xavier, Nina, Ramon, Marta and Marcos – children of the founder.

Note:
In 1958, Enric Bernat introduced the first round-shaped lollipop in the Spanish market under the Chupa Chups brand name (manufactured by Granja Asturias). In 1964, the company changed its name to SA CHUPA CHUPS. In 1969, Salvador Dalí contributed to the brand logo design and, in the 1970s, the company started its internationalisation. New brands – Smint and Crazy Planet – were launched in 1994 and 1998 respectively. The group's excellence has been recognised by different institutions around the world. It has received several awards, among them: the "European Candy Kettle" in 1986, the "Prince Felipe Award for Business Excellency in Internationalisation" in 1997. At the Cannes Festival in June 2001, Smint was awarded the "Silver Lions Award" for outdoor advertising.

Enric Bernat Fontlladosa to his children

To My Dear Children,

Three years have gone by since I resigned as President of our company, Chupa Chups S.A., and gave the Board of Administrators the task of appointing all of you to new posts, which was definitely not an easy task. Nevertheless, it was clear to me all along that if I wanted the best for you all, I had to wait until all five of you had reached consensus on the matter.

In the fifty years I managed the company, you always were involved in the day-to-day business and occupied executive posts. Still, I have to admit that you relied too much on the fact that your father was always there behind the scenes. Now, after letting your decision mature for three years, and following criteria of your own choosing, you have decided to withdraw from executive management, but remain on the governing board and appoint professional managers for the company. This was an intelligent decision – you have taken a step forward for the generations to come.

Always try to bear in mind what your parents, in all modesty, have done: we have loved you dearly and respected your opinions. That's how we have managed to keep us united for fifty years of joy and prosperity. As each of you reached adulthood, we gave you 10% of the family patrimony in order to create a bond with it. Obviously, as each of you came into the family business, your characters started taking shape. During this period, to keep you all united, I had many long conversations with your mother, deciding, in some cases, to create related companies for some of you to manage or, in other cases, distributing separate responsibilities in the family business.

Today, after fifty years, you meet every week to discuss the management of the company; each quarter, together with two external counsellors and the CEO, we have an administration council. The personal wish of your parents, who founded the business, is that you fill the space in your own lives in whatever way allows you to be happy and to enjoy work as we always have – this will be the key to your happiness.

The purpose of a business should be to create wealth, prosperity and happiness for all family members. You know I always say, "satisfaction comes from a job well done." Time will tell whether we, the founders, have been wise in preparing the future and the continuity of Chupa Chups, our family business.

Papa

2

SIBLINGS

Founders of businesses often entrust the business to their children, hoping that the children will work as a team. It is common, in fact, for founders to distribute ownership equally among the siblings, but appoint one as the next leader. Think of this system as "first among equals." This form of succession works well when one of the siblings is a trusted and respected leader (Qian Hu), or when the siblings grew up as a true team and share deep love and a sense of togetherness (Strauss), but it is not always easy.

Siblings often have some difficulty reporting to another sibling, especially when they are equal owners and have equal representation on the company board. When one sibling enjoys the power of a higher position the others do not share, tensions and conflicts among siblings can arise. When some siblings work in the business and others don't, both parties may feel the discrepancy in power even more strongly. They may have diverging views on compensation, dividend policies and investments for the business. In the absence of good communication and relationships that help them cope with the stress generated by these differences of opinion, sibling teams may fall victim to more envy, rivalry and feuds than the family would like to see.

An alternative to the first-among-equals model is shared leadership. The Puig Corporation in Spain, for instance, can boast of team leadership: four brothers in the second generation have been working together for forty-five years. Shared leadership like this works well when siblings are committed to unity and harmony and share a common vision and values. On the down side, however, depending on how efficiently the team members work together,

17

shared leadership can slow down decision-making, since, for each major decision, the members of the team must reach consensus.

The successful siblings teams we have observed, whether they fit the shared-leadership model or first-among-equals model, build on their differences. They complement one another and use their different skills and talents as a strength for their relationship and for the business.

Strauss-Elite Ltd.

Location: Israel

Turnover (in US$): $862 million (2000)

Date of exchange rate: December 2000

Name of local currency: Israeli Shekel (NIS)

Number of employees: 6340 (2000)

Activity/industry sector: Dairy, salads, ice-cream, chocolate, coffee

Geographic spread of the business: Israel, Brazil, East Europe

Year the business was started: 1936

Name of the founder and relation to the author: Hilda & Richard Strauss, parents

Generation running the business: 3rd

Name & position of person writing the letter: Raya Strauss-Bendror, owner

Other family members active in the business: Ofra Strauss-Lahat, chairwoman, Strauss-Elite; Adi Strauss, vice managing director, Elite International

% of capital owned by the family: 100%

Recipient(s) of the letter: all members of the 3rd generation

Note:
When Hilda and Richard Strauss left Germany for Israel in 1936, they purchased a plot of land in Nahariya and on it built their house and a small cowshed and started a farm, with one cow. They tried to sell the milk to their neighbours, but the task was not easy. People were not used to drinking fresh milk. So, with the surplus of milk, Hilda started making cheese, and was soon concocting her own recipes. Two years later, Hilda started harvesting strawberries in a nearby field and created a strawberries and cream desert that became famous all over the north of Israel. In 1939, the Strausses sold their twenty cows and founded the Strauss Dairy, Nahariya.

By 1949, the Dairy employed a handful of workers, and Hilda made her first attempts at producing ice-cream. Competition was fierce – the Strauss Dairy had to fight against two individual dairies and two monopolies. Investing all their money to grow the dairy and acquire production equipment, and getting no subsidies from the government, the Strauss Dairy Hilda was threatened several times by closure.

In 1956, Michael Strauss, their son, joined the business. Their daughter, Raya, decided for a career outside the family business, though her husband, Vevel, worked at the plant. It was only in 1977 that Raya joined the business as Michael's personal assistant.

Michael brought long term planning, sales strategy and marketing methods into the business. He worked relentlessly to grow the company and make it profitable. At the end of the nineteen fifties, the Strauss dairies employed three hundred people. The company entered a partnership with the French company Gervais Danone, and stopped producing hard and processed cheeses to enter the era of dairy desserts. Thanks to the quality of their products, the commitment of their employees, the personal relationships they built with their clients, and their determination, the Strauss family gradually managed to enter monopoly markets such as Tel-Aviv and Jerusalem.

In the early 1990s, the Strauss family re-organized the company and decided to diversify away from dairy products. For this purpose, they founded the Gideon Holding Company to developing new businesses outside the sphere of dairy. Acquisitions included a salad production company, a ready made pasta plant, pasta sauces, a chain of six restaurants, ice-cream shops, a participation in TV channel franchises and many others.

In September 1995, Strauss signed 50% of its ice-cream factory over to Unilever and in return got vital knowledge and brands. In February 1996, Gideon Holding acquired 25% of Elite, Israel's largest chocolate and food producer. Michael was hesitant at first, but Raya and Ofra – Michael's daughter and closest associate in charge of new business development – convinced him that food production was a unique opportunity.

At a family meeting, it was decided that in the year 2000, Ofra would be appointed Chairwoman of the Strauss factories. Along with her brother Adi, Director General of the commercial chains, and her cousin Gili, responsible for new business development in the dairy department, Ofra has successfully worked her way up the Strauss ladder, proving her competence and trustworthiness. Nava, Irit and Rany, the other three members of the third generation, have opted for careers outside the family business. Nava is a co-owner of a toy factory that exports, imports and produces toys; Irit is a partner in a publicity firm; and Rany has chosen an artistic career. The three of them support all Strauss activities.

Today, the Strauss Dairies are modern and sophisticated production plants, with an entire fleet of trucks that distributes 120 types of dairy products each day all over Israel every day. It employs twelve hundred people operating twenty four hours a day, six days a week.

Source: Levi S. Y. (1998). *Strausse – The Story of a Family and of an Industry.* Jerusalem, Israel: Keter Publishing House.

Raya Strauss-Ben-Dror to her children, nephew and nieces

This is an occasion to pass on to you – Nava, Ofra, Gili, Irit, Adi and Rani, members of the third generation – something of the spark and essence of the togetherness that has continued like a scarlet thread from our parents and right on down to Michael and me. It is impossible to describe the history of Strauss without tying mother and father together. Mother's special qualities complemented father's amazing personality: they were a single unit, a team, and their achievements were shared achievements.

It all began in their early childhoods, when each of them, for their own reasons, decided to build a family on the foundation of togetherness, something they had never known in their parents' homes. Father grew up in a family that lived in disharmony, without togetherness, communication, or flow. Life at home was conducted around his rigid father Julius, who had great expectations of each of his four children, which they struggled to meet. Father's mother, Martha, was different. Many years younger than Julius, she loved laughter and the good life. Having been born and raised in the Rhine region, under French influence, had had a great impact on her character. Julius, by contrast, had been born and raised in southern Germany, and was far stricter and more conservative than she. Father, a smart and sensitive child, suffered greatly from the fact that his parents barely communicated, and decided, while still a boy, to have a different family.

In contrast to father's parents, mother's parents, Bertha and Fritz Bach, shared a great togetherness. They loved each other very much, and were a single, inseparable unit. Fritz, orphaned by his mother's death, had grown up in the shadow of a stepmother who did not love him. When he met Bertha, he became completely devoted to her. She was beautiful, the spoiled youngest child in a family of ten children in a branch of the Rothschild family. In those days, children were raised by a governess; mother had virtually no contact with her parents, and decided that her children would be part of a family unit. Her children, like her husband, would always come first.

Many years later mother and father met at a Hannuka ball organized by the Jewish community in Ulm. It was love at first sight. They decided to bind their fates: they would build a togetherness that would be different from what they had known in their parents' homes. Mother documented their lives before marriage in a diary, and in it, she describes an intense, great love that overcame all obstacles. Because the two were young, their families placed many hurdles between them. Mother was trundled off to a prestigious boarding school for young ladies in Switzerland to keep her apart from father, who was sent to the university in Tübingen. In those days there were no fax machines, and they had no phones at their disposal, so they traded long letters in which they shared their great love. In April 1933, their love prevailed – they were married. Michael was born one year later, and two years later, they immigrated to Israel. Both were Zionists, both had been members of the Zionist youth movement Blau Weiss, and both were determined to build their home and future in Israel.

Life in Israel was not easy. Father never acclimatized, for he always missed "there." From the first moment, however, mother envisioned Israel as her home. "The last Moroccan in Israel is closer to me," she told me, "than any German in Ulm." Father struggled his whole life between being a true Zionist and working man, and his failure to fit with the Israeli mentality. He was a European German lost in the Levant. He never managed to accept the orientation of might, the lack of professionalism and the rudeness. He never understood the Israeli mind. "Everything I have learned, all my degrees are worth nothing in Israel," he always said. "Everything that is true all over the world is not true here."

Mother and father were truly a mirror of Germanness. To the end of their days they never learned to speak Hebrew properly. They spoke to us as well as to their friends and acquaintances in German. They were very cultured people. When they got together with their friends in Nahariya, they listened to classical music and read poetry together. When mother entertained guests for dinner, she mixed cards on which she wrote the beginning or end of quotes from Goethe or Schiller, and the guests had to find their dinner partner by correctly pairing the cards. Mother was a woman of words. Father, all soul and emotion, had less of a way with words. He was unable to express his feelings and did not engage in heart-to-heart conversations.

Still, Michael remembers three occasions on which father did speak, in his own special way. When Michael told father that he wanted to be a seaman, father – despite wanting Michael to stay with Strauss – not only expressed no objection whatsoever, he went with him by bus and enrolled him at the Naval Academy. When Michael was a cadet at the Naval Academy and was about to sail abroad for the first time in his life, father took him aside and told him, "You are about to encounter something you do not know – prostitutes. When my brother Rudi was a student, he went to one and caught syphilis. He went through hell, and I don't know if the disease doesn't have any implications on the illnesses from which he suffers today. So I'm relying on you to use your good sense, whether to go to a woman like that or not." On that trip and others Michael took around the world, when his friends went to wherever they went, Michael went elsewhere. That's how much father's words had meant to him. Lastly, when Michael and father were in Germany with Velvel, father said, "I'm not sure that Raya and Velvel's marriage will last much longer, and I want your word of honor now, that after I'm gone you will take care of Raya." Michael gave father his word of honor, and as you know, he has kept it for each and every moment of our lives together.

Father and I shared a great closeness, a spiritual bond that was true telepathy. He was not a man of great words with me either, but there was no need for words between us; we saw everything in each other's eyes. He always gave me the feeling that he trusted me, and thanks to him, I feel very sheltered to this very day.

Father was a rare, special man. A man of vision, he believed in peace and did not know the nature of hatred. Despite what the Germans had done, he never hated Germany, and when the idea was born of Germany atoning for its sins against the Jewish people by reparations, he saw it as an opportunity for words and did everything to bridge the two countries. For this activity, he was officially honored by the German government. He was one of the first Jews to host Germans in Israel. He was proud to host his teacher, Professor Heuss, who by then had become President of the Republic of West Germany. Father was also a man of peace and forgiveness. He believed equally in peace with our neighbors, the Arabs. He loved Arabs and had Arab friends whose homes he visited, just as they visited ours. Yasser Arafat's deputy, Abu Ma'azen, once told us that during the Mandate, father had done business with his father, who owned goat herds, and that they had shared a relationship of mutual respect.

Father taught Michael and me to respect a man as a man, regardless of religion, race or nationality. He was not a materialistic person and invested almost everything he earned in Strauss. He was always giving money to others, always helping needy widows and orphans and anyone else who came to him for help. He was an honest man, somewhat naive, who on more than one occasion was exploited because of his guilelessness. He felt uncomfortable in the company of the rich, and found things much easier with the simple folk. He loved the workers at the factory and always cared for them. The first thing he did when he received reparations from Germany was to give the workers a free meal and, at a time when no one even dreamed of doing so, played soothing background music in the factory.

Father loved to entertain. Sometimes, without warning, he came home with a bunch of people and asked mother to prepare a meal for them. Mother shed more than a few tears over these "surprises," but she never said no. Father was a philosopher, an intellectual, who took an interest in the spiritual. Decades before it became fashionable, he took an interest in astrology, in reading coffee grinds and tarot cards. He was an open man, a bohemian who was attracted to special people. For years he was the patron of Eli Avivi, and he greatly loved to spend vacations at Rafi Nelson's village.

On more than one occasion father's creative personality led to practical solutions that propelled Strauss forward. For example, when Gervais sued us for use of its brand name, instead of fighting a war, father suggested a peaceful solution and thus reached a know-how agreement with Gervais that entirely altered the course of Strauss's history.

The union of mother and father was a winning combination…he a dreamer, and she practical, he sensitive and vulnerable, she tougher. When he had had enough of government bureaucracy and what he called the imperviousness of "our good friends," he sent mother to the authorities instead of going himself. Mother wouldn't move until she got what she wanted. She was committed to father, and never dreamed of letting him down. Father always believed in mother's unique abilities; and he also believed in women's abilities to take responsibility for different areas of life. And he, who lived in a time when men sent women to the kitchen, imposed upon her tasks that were then only imposed on men: she traveled to Jerusalem and to Tel Aviv at a time when Nahariya was considered the end of the world. She traveled on his missions abroad, bought machines, knocked on the doors of banks and institutions, spending hours in the hallways, waiting for the right official, who, usually indifferent and patronizing, would let her wait sometimes for days. But she never gave up, and whenever father asked, she went back again and again and again.

And always, both for father and mother, above everything else came the family. Michael and I grew up in this togetherness, and it has accompanied us throughout our lives. Michael was born in a difficult time: he emigrated with our parents from Germany to Israel, and then from Beer Tuvia to Nahariya. He was with them when they settled on the land, when they toiled to build their lives in the new country. He absorbed the hardships and the pain. I was already born into the routine of a life planted deep in the earth, but even I experienced the sufferings at the beginning of the way.

You, members of the third generation, were born into security, at the beginning of the path that led us to success. You were born almost into the ready-made. You were spared the hardships of the beginning, the problems of making a living, the inner struggles, the difficulty, the tough competition that Strauss faced in the early years. You, like Strauss, are the source of our pride. We place our trust in you and are handing you the heritage of the home of father and mother. After mother's death we found a letter in which she wrote: "It is most important to me that after we have gone, the sense of unity will be preserved in the family, the desire to be together, that there will be peace in our family." This is our heritage of togetherness. Mother always said, "One cannot fight both inward and outward." And today Michael and I are passing on to you the magic formula: stay together, and hold on to the assets that are dearest to us of all, the family and the business.

We have done what we were charged to do. Today, we are signing an agreement in the spirit of mother's legacy, an agreement that will enable each of you to choose your own way, but at the same time, to preserve our togetherness. Your mission is more difficult than our parents' and ours. So far, experience has shown that members of the first and second generations succeed in preserving the togetherness. But members of the third generation who have succeeded in doing so are few. And therefore, more will be demanded of you: more decision, more determination, more love and more faith. I believe in you. I believe that you will achieve the impossible.

Raya

Raya Strauss-Ben-Dror

Business partner and Board member

Strauss Dairies

Radio Flyer Inc.

Location: Chicago, IL, USA

Number of employees: 100

Activity/industry sector: Toys

Geographic spread of the business: USA, Canada, Japan, some Europe

Year the business was started: 1917

Name of the founder and relation to the author: Antonio Pasin, grandfather of the author

Generation running the business: 3rd

Name & position of person writing the letter: Robert Pasin, President & CEO

Other family members active in the business: Paul Pasin, brother, executive vice-president

Recipient(s) of the letter: Helen (6) and Henry (2), children of the author

Note:
Radio Flyer Inc, like the original little red wagon from which it got its name, is an American classic. Since its founding in 1917, under the management of each three generations of the Pasin family, Radio Flyer has crafted millions of toys that lift children's imaginations.

It all started with Antonio Pasin, the Italian immigrant boy who bought some wood working tools and started hand-crafting wooden wagons in a one-room shop in Chicago. Business grew, and by 1923 he had hired a helper and called his venture the Liberty Coaster Company, a name he borrowed from the Statue of Liberty. Soon his traditional handcrafting could not keep pace with demand, so he started applying mass production techniques to wagon-making.

By 1930, the company, newly named Radio Steel & Manufacturing, had become the world's largest producer of coaster wagons. Through the Great Depression, when the company made more than 1500 wagons a day, and into the 1930s, the company never closed it doors. But in 1941, the US government rationed steel, and Radio Steel & Manufacturing workers went off to war. After the armistice, however, millions of Americans moved to the suburbs, buying houses and pursuing their personal dreams. Growing families meant an upswing in the demand for wagons, and it also ushered in the second generation of the Pasin family, Antonio's son who, as President and CEO, led the company to produce an innovative line of garden carts, and eventually wheel-barrows.

Now, Antonio's grandchildren, the third generation of Pasins, have taken over operations and are developing new products. They remain dedicated to the company's long tradition of quality, safety and service, still feeling a sense of responsibility for the millions of children who play with their products: metal edges are rolled under to prevent scratching, and the red paint is harmless. Today, Radio Flyer is the world's leading producer of toy wagons—from hand-crafted wood wagons, to stamped steel wagons, and to the latest in all, plastic wagons. The 80 year old dream is still alive and driving the family.

Robert Pasin, President & CEO of Radio Flyer Inc.

Robert Pasin to his children

Dear Helen & Henry,

Our family business is built on dreams. It began with the implausible dream of a 16-year old immigrant who literally had little more than a dream for a better life. Your great grandfather, Antonio Pasin, or "Nonno," did what it is almost impossible for me to imagine. In 1914, as a boy of 16, he left his home, his family, and his entire world, as he knew it in Rosa, Italy to come to America – the promised land of opportunity. What caused him to make this decision? I wish so much that I could ask him that question, but by the time I was old enough to ask, Nonno's senility had rendered him unable to answer.

While we may never know exactly all the reasons for his decision, we do know that your great grandfather had a dream, and he overcame many obstacles to reach it. In one sense, his dream was quite simple – to work in America until he had enough money to go home to Rosa to make a better life for himself and his family. Nonno had no idea how complex and difficult a path he had chosen. Nor did he have any idea that he would live the rest of his life in America, raise three children here, and build a company and toy that have become American icons.

After numerous jobs on the west side of Chicago – he hauled water for road construction crews and worked at the Kimball piano factory, among other things – Antonio set off to start his own business making phonograph cabinets. Although his new venture, the Venetian Furniture Company did pretty well, Nonno was soon getting more requests from customers for the wooden wagons he had built to haul tools around his workshop. He had named the first such wagon the Liberty Coaster for the Statue of Liberty that had welcomed him to America. Soon he changed the cabinet production line so that he could work with steel and start mass producing his little red wagons. The Radio Flyer was born!

How was he able to start his own business in 1917 and prosper? He was passionate about his dream. No one could take that away. He was a skilled carpenter with a great talent for beautiful design; time and again, he used that skill to better his status in the workplace. Antonio was a hard worker, and his personal integrity and honesty were bedrock. His big, warm, winning smile made people love him and trust him. These I believe were the basic ingredients of his success.

Many years later, by the time I was 11 years old, Nonno's senility was so advanced that I barely knew him. And you will never know him. What can we learn from his life journey? I have learned that I must follow my dreams. Life is about discovering your heart's desire and pursuing it vigorously. I have learned that if you love your work you will be happy. I have learned that personal integrity and faith are among our greatest gifts; they must never be tarnished.

Since the moment I set foot on the factory floor at the age of 5, I have been fascinated by this business. Radio Flyer is all about dreams and creativity, all of which began with Nonno's vision. We create products that unleash children's dreams. That little red wagon is a race car or a space ship or a time travel machine. People have an emotional bond with our products – they had one of our little red wagons when they were kids, and they want their kids to have one, too. These are the magical qualities of a little red wagon. And these are the things that inspire and motivate me. The potential also compels me – what can Radio Flyer become? I'm just getting started!

Helen and Henry, although you are only six and two, one day you will read this letter. I want you to know when you do that you should always follow *your* dreams, just as your great grandfather followed his. And just as I did. Never follow *his* dreams. Never follow *my* dreams. You must pursue your own. Of course, I would be delighted if the next generation of Pasins kept running the company and we have developed a succession policy through our family meetings for your generation to be part of Radio Flyer. But you should only come into the business if you are one hundred percent convinced that it is one of your dreams. If you follow your dreams, true happiness and success will follow and I will be the proudest father in the world.

Love,

Poppy

Qian Hu Corporation Limited

Location: Singapore

Turnover (in US$): 22.5 million (2001)

Number of employees: 187

Activity/industry sector: Import/export of ornamental fish; manufacture and distribution of aquarium accessories

Geographic spread of the business: Export to more than 54 countries. Subsidiaries in Thailand, Malaysia, and China.

Year the business was started: 1989

Name & position of person writing the letter: Kenny Yap, Chairman and CEO, Co-Founder.

Other family members active in the business: Four older brothers and two cousins.

% of capital owned by the family: 80%

Recipient(s) of the letter: Kenny Yap's 12 nieces and 6 nephews

Note:
When the Singapore government decided to diversify away from the traditional farming industry, the Yap family (Kenny Yap's father and elder brothers) transformed their pig farm into fish ponds. They initially started with the breeding and distribution of guppies, and later expanded the range to include ornamental fish. In 1990, they started a local wholesale distribution business, and in 1992, they decided to import and export ornamental fish and aquarium accessories. 1993 was the year of international expansion, with the opening of a subsidiary in China. Later, another subsidiary was opened in Thailand, and distribution in Malaysia was expanded. In December 1998, Qian Hu farm was incorporated. Since taking over the business in 1995, Kenny Yap's motivation has been to modernise the company, diversify and raise standards. He has transformed the business into a multinational that today exports directly to more than 54 countries. Qian Hu was the first industrial company in Singapore to achieve ISO 9002, and in recent years received several awards, such as the Singapore Entrepreneur of the year (1996 and 1998), the International Europe Award for Quality (1999), several Aquarama Fish Competition Medals and the 2001 Star of Asia Entrepreneurs by Business Week. Qian Hu's belief is that "lives should be treasured and cherished" and their philosophy is to "bring fun and versatile lives" to their customers.

Kenny Yap to his nieces and nephews

My Dear Nephews and Nieces,

I view all of you as the third generation of our family. Although our ornamental fish and aquarium accessories business is technically in the first generation – after all, your grandfather was a pig farmer, and we are fish farmers now – the nature of our family business now, its culture of unity and cohesiveness is, in fact, second generation because both your fathers and I learned from your late grandfather how important it is to stick together during ups and downs.

Many family businesses fail, especially after the third generation, because they take family members into the business based on relationship, not ability. One of the reasons Qian Hu Corporation Limited is doing fine now is that we are passionate: we do the things we love, and we want to use our abilities to help the business succeed. Unless you have the same passion and ability, unless you can put the company first, not your individual needs, we will not allow you to join us. Just take your parent shares, remain as shareholders, and pursue your own dreams.

Meanwhile study hard and equip yourselves with knowledge and skills. These will be yours, regardless of whether you join us later or not. No matter what happens, whether you work in our family business or you pursue your own career, you are always our dear family members, and I will always be your uncle by blood.

Uncle Kenny

3

COUSINS

When families in business reach the third or subsequent generations, they enter the most complex stage of all, the cousins stage. By this time, the family is usually large, and has several branches. Few family members are involved in the operations, as is the case with Paulig. The business can be in a mature stage, like Algar, with a large number of employees and subsidiaries, and multiple divisions. Ownership is usually fragmented, and normally, no single owner has enough power to sway strategic decisions. Well-known examples of families in business that have reached this stage are Cargill in the USA with a turnover of US$ 49 billion (2001) and 90,000 employees; the almost 200 year-old Bonnier Group in Sweden with some 65 family owners[4] or the Mulliez group in France, which we shall hear from later in this book, with 475 family associates and 850 family members.

A good governance structure can manage this complexity by clearly separating family issues, business issues and ownership issues, and also improving communication among the family members (De Agostini). Putting such a structure in place can require painstaking and time- consuming efforts, but it can also reward the family with clear answers to thorny questions, among them: Who will own shares? Can shares be sold? If so, under what conditions? Who is entitled to enter the business? Who can sit on the company board?

The cousins stage can also provide diverse opportunities for family members: jobs in the business, involvement in the family council, family trusts or foundations, responsibility for family charities, or, because ownership provides regular income and dividends, even freedom of career choice.

One of the key difficulties of the cousins stage is that, since family members may live apart, many of them are disconnected from the business, and, at times, from the family. The family usually has to take a lot of time to build bonds, foster shareholders' loyalty to the business and the family values, and train shareholders to be responsible and committed owners (Maus). Further, since more owners are not working in the business, and may depend on dividends for at least part of their income, there is often a higher need for dividends. At the same time, the business itself may need resources to grow and expand. It is thus crucial that family members find a good balance between the needs of the family and the needs of the business and acknowledge and respect their different wishes, career paths and interests. With this balance, they stand a good chance of staying on the road to success.

'Karlsson Stider, A. (2000). "Family and Firm." Doctoral dissertation. Sweden.

Maus Frères S.A.

Location: Geneva, Switzerland

Turnover (in US$): Approx. $1.2 billion

Date of exchange rate: March 5, 2002

Name of local currency: Swiss Francs

Number of employees: 15,000

Activity/industry sector: retail

Geographic spread of the business: All Switzerland (Maus) – worldwide (Devanlay, holding of Lacoste, 90% family-owned)

Year the business was started: 1902

Name of the founder and relation to the interviewee: Léon Nordmann, grandfather

Generation running the business: 4th (3rd generation still present at board level)

Name & position of person interviewed: Philippe Nordmann, president of the board

Other family members active in the business: Didier Maus, Thierry Halff, Olivier Maus, Pierre-André Maus

Other family members non-active shareholders: Maryse Gentinetta-Nordmann, Marie-Laure Rondeau-Maus, Nathalie Sommer-Maus, Nathalie Barthe-Nordmann, Serge Nordmann, Laurence Cheneau-Halff, Pascal Nordmann, Isabelle Nordmann, Alexandra Fabert-Maus, Marion Moatti-Maus.

% of capital owned by the family: 100% (50% Maus family, 50% Nordmann family)

Philippe Nordmann

It all began with three friends: Léon Nordmann and Ernest and Henri Maus. Léon Nordmann opened a department store in 1902 in Willisau (Lucerne, Switzerland) and that was the beginning of the story of 70 department stores in Switzerland. The brothers Ernest and Henri Maus were hosiery and haberdashery wholesalers who supplied goods to their friend Nordmann, and rapidly went into partnership with the department stores.

In 1929, Léon Nordmann married his son, Robert (my father), to Ernest's daughter, Simone, which united the two families, and is why our shops are called "Manor," from the first letters of the names Maus and Nordmann. Since 1929, the families have shared the partnership 50:50.

Management Succession

From the beginning, the management of the business has been passed on only to male members of the families who have reached the age of 30, and only if they are considered worthy and capable. Female members do not work in the business. This rule has always been accepted well by the family. Until the third generation, all the worthy and capable male members worked in it. Now that we are in the fourth generation and the family is getting larger, we will have to be stricter. And the women, if they are considered worthy and capable, will also probably be able to take on management positions. Certain members, such as my son, who is an actor and director ("metteur en scène"), have chosen not to go into the business. He and the others are non-active shareholders.

Governance System

For a short time – since only two years – two external (non-family) members on our Board of Directors have sat on our the team of four executive shareholders. The two are in banking and industry. We chose them for their expertise in our business and their human qualities. Their presence enriches our meetings. So far as managing the business goes, none of the divisional directors is a family member. The four active members of the family are directors of the holding company. In the future, however, a member of the family may well join the management at the business level.

We have a shareholders' committee that, in addition to the Annual General Meeting, meets twice a year. We recently appointed a non-active shareholder to act as go-between for the executive shareholders and the non-active shareholders. Although we do not yet have a family council, we are considering calling all the adult members of the family together to try to strengthen the ties among us.

Growth of the Business

Four years ago, we acquired Devanlay which, at that time, was manufacturing Lacoste products. We had been looking for a long time for a group to acquire. Some groups were too large; others were too small. We particularly wanted a company we could develop. At that time, Lacoste was a traditional label, a bit outdated, and we have invested a lot to build it up. We have given the image a younger look, expanded the collection by adding sportswear and city wear (shirts, pullovers, parkas, trousers) and men's underwear. Above all, we are extending the range of clothes for women and children. We took over design and distribution from "Chemises Lacoste", so Devanlay is now the designer, manufacturer and distributor of Lacoste products worldwide. The Lacoste label is now selling very well.

Rules for Entering the Business

In the future, a member of the family who is not capable will not be employed simply because he is his father's son. We do not have a family charter or written rules for determining who is worthy and capable. The appraisal is made by the preceding generation, based on their experience. After observing the person in business training for two or three years, they can normally say if that person is worthy and capable or not. Before joining the group, all executive shareholders are also required to work abroad, outside the family business.

Generally the members of the family have a lot of respect for each other and a great regard for the process of evaluating who is worthy and capable of joining the group. That does not mean, however, that we have never had any painful situations when we have had to bar certain members of the family from entering the business. In such cases, what keeps the family together is the longevity of the business. It is our hard and fast rule that everything must be governed by the principle of company continuity.

Members of the family have always entered the business with the idea of reaching a top position very quickly. Theoretically, it is possible that a member with different skills – design, communications, human relations – could enter the company at another level, but it has never happened.

Transition Between Generations

From 1929 to 1945, for 16 years, the first and second generations (my grandfather and my father) worked together. Contrasted with other companies, that is a long time. For the 29 years between 1960 and 1989, the third and fourth generations worked side by side. The transition between the third and fourth generations lasted 11 years from 1990 to 2001. Because succeeding generations have worked side-by-side for so long, we have been able to pass on our wide experience, our ways of working and our values.

I think we have always had a very good way of working. We have tried to give members of the younger generation maximum independence to run the business while we, the previous generation, remain available to give them the benefit of our experience. Except when the younger generation have taken disproportionately large risks, we have never held them back.

Settling Disagreements

Even if we have always worked well together during the transitions from generation to generation, we have, of course, not always agreed. When there is a difference of opinion, however, there is always a flashing signal to remind us of our guiding principle: the perennity of our family business. Everyone tries to remember the question, "How can we best achieve continuity?" That is how we come to an agreement.

We are now in the fourth generation, and we have a very strong company culture. We have learned to work together; many ties have been passed from generation to generation. Having seen so many family businesses collapse – Eaton in Canada and Gallerias Preciados in Spain, for example – we understand that in order to continue it is essential to be united. And to achieve that union, we have to exclude from the business people who are too individualistic.

Transfer of Ownership

Shares have been transferred from generation to generation, respecting the 50:50 rule, to each male or female descendant. Each shareholder may therefore hold a different number of shares, but the overall shareholdings of the two families are equal. Traditionally, the wives receive shares from their husbands only when the latter die, and on the condition that the shares will pass to their children. Since we consider it imperative to keep the members of the family updated regularly, during the transition between the third and fourth generations, we introduced twice-yearly training sessions for the non-active shareholders.

There are no preferred shares. Whether the shareholders are active or not, they all hold the same type of shares. In any case, we do not vote. In the 100 years our business has existed, we have never needed to vote at the executive shareholder level. We do hold an annual general meeting every year, but everyone always agrees to the decisions taken. The family is informed in advance, and if there are objections, they are put forward. We always take decisions together bearing in mind the perennity of the business.

The majority of the shares are transferred to the next generation when a death occurs. However, to encourage their children the older generation can transfer partial shareholdings. My father did that with my brother and me, and I have done it with my children.

Family Values

Our attitude as a family in the company towards the business has always been to attach great importance to human beings, both in the family and in the department stores. We consider training to be very important: we devote 60,000 hours per year to it.

Social Responsibility

As a company, we take part in several social service activities: we support the arts, but are also very open to humanitarian causes. We were the first to deliver aid to the boat people (Vietnam), and, after earthquakes, transported food and clothing to people in the affected areas of Kurdistan and to orphanages in Romania. We also contribute a considerable sum each year for aid at Christmas: in 2001 we supported the Theodora organisation, clowns who entertain children in hospital.

We take a great interest in the environment. We were the first in Switzerland, for example, to show concern about packaging and batteries. We also have a charter of ethics that we apply to purchasing; amongst other things, the charter precludes us from buying from entities that employ child labour. The charter is more than the mere written word – we regularly send people to verify that our suppliers are honouring our policy. The entities in question know we are monitoring them, and our agents' visits have a dissuasive effect.

We are also active in the Philias foundation, whose aim is to promote the social service role of companies, to help them fulfil it, and to make management realise that not only profit counts. In our business, we are acutely aware of our obligation for social service. As a family we do not have joint projects for this kind of activity. All the members of the family invest their time and money as they wish in the charities they support.

The Future

We are not planning to become a publicly-owned company. I believe that the family brings a lot to our business. The members of the family feel responsible. The executive shareholders have a triple responsibility: towards the business, towards the employees, and towards the other members of the family. Also, a family business has one undeniable advantage over other businesses: thanks to rapid decision making it can react quickly.

If I have a wish for the business it is that it may continue in the hands of the family for several more generations. Even if it is still too early to predict its future, the fifth generation is already 23 strong, with ages ranging from 3 months to 16 years.

Philippe Nordmann

Chairman

Maus Frères

Switzerland

De Agostini S.p.A.

Location: Novara, Italy

Turnover (in US$): $1 billion (2001)

Date of exchange rate: March 30, 2002

Name of local currency: Italian Lire

Number of employees: 3,000

Activity/industry sector: Publishing

Geographic spread of the business: Operations in 33 countries around the world

Year the business was started: 1901

Name of the founder and relation to the author: Giovanni De Agostini - not related

Generation running the business: 3rd

Name & position of person writing the letter: Marco Drago, CEO

Other family members active in the business: 7 first cousins at various levels in the business

Other family members non-active shareholders: 15

% of capital owned by the family: 100%

Recipient(s) of the letter: children of the author: Marcella (30), editor – Enrico (25) and Nicola (24), students

Note:
The families Boroli and Drago own the business. They have been shareholders since 1919.

Marco Drago to his children

Dearest Marcella, Enrico, and Nicola,

At this moment I feel the need to collect and set out, in some order, the most significant ideas and reflections that have come up in our recent chats regarding your future relations with the family business. So, the primary purpose of my letter is to contribute to the evaluation framework (above all psychological, I hope) that you are creating for yourselves autonomously in order to decide whether or not you will be interested in joining the already numerous partners who work in the company. I am convinced of the importance of making this decision only after careful consideration and thoughtful reflection.

I won't dwell on the reasons that may influence your decision to continue being shareholders in a company of which, sooner or later (I hope later), you will possess a stake of little more than one per cent, together with fifty or so members of our family, and which has now happily reached its fourth generation.

To hold on to success, you must grow. In the business world, you can't stay in one place; you either move ahead or fall behind. And to move ahead, the company must know how to continually and rapidly evolve, more quickly than its competitors and as far as possible, with one goal: creating material value. In the pursuit of this goal, family members completely control our company capital. Such family control is partially true with regard to carrying out the entrepreneurial role, and for the most part, untrue in the management of the company, where professional and family managers work together productively. In developing our business in recent years, this last point has been particularly crucial.

Projecting this analysis into the future, it is certain that, to continue to progress successfully, the company must necessarily give more and more space to professional managers, reliable and qualified, who will have to work in complete harmony with the owners. The owners, for their part, will play the role of representing the shareholders, with clear intentions, unity of direction, and effective control. In this way, among other things, the shareholders will continue to receive the maximum return on their capital.

For this reason, in time, the space reserved for shareholders in the running of the company will possibly diminish. However, it is essential that at least a certain number of shareholders, both inside and outside the company, have all the necessary experience to qualify them as points of reference in representing the rest of the shareholders. Simply put, in order for everything to work in the best possible way, we need a highly skilled management team that can carry on a dialogue with well-informed and competent shareholders.

Personally, I do not advise you to work in the family business if you have to live with secondary responsibilities that will remain secondary into the future. The reality is that, initially, in a work situation, value must be placed on such considerations as peace of mind and job security, aspects that are not to be disregarded. In time, however, anyone with the slightest bit of ambition and a normal desire for professional achievement will probably become extremely dissatisfied. The individual, being a shareholder and bearer of a certain surname, will to a lesser or greater extent begin to think he has not made enough of a name for himself and so will feel diminished in his own eyes, those of his family, and those of the other shareholders.

Naturally, becoming a top-level manager, much less "commander in chief," is not necessary, but it seems important to me that you put yourselves in a position to understand whether or not the conditions exist to allow you to avoid feeling that you are "one of many." (This would depend on both you and the company.) In other words, I believe the essential thing is that you keep, as much as possible, motivational mechanisms intact. This is what will allow you to get what you want out of your work experience.

But what, then, are the characteristics and the qualities needed to succeed in a family business?

First of all, there are those qualities that make up the conditions for success in any company. I won't list them here, because too many books have already been written on the subject. But I would simply like to emphasize how, in our situation, it is especially crucial that these qualities be accompanied by a healthy dose of a spirit of sacrifice, a great capacity for relating to people, discussing, and mediating, together with a vision for the medium- and long-term. In other words, two sets of principles must be made to coexist: those of good management and those of family agreement and unity. As a result, the required effort is doubled.

If you choose to actively commit to the family business, great advantages and considerable satisfaction await you: working for yourself (for your own investment, I mean to say), together with other family members and professional managers in an atmosphere of collaboration and serenity, confirmed by positive results. These factors probably make up one of the most favourable and constructive work situations one could aspire to. In my opinion it's right, then, that – all conditions being equal – the company expect greater dedication and deeper commitment from shareholder-managers.

Beyond this, knowing you have contributed decisively to ferrying the company across the river from one generation to the other can be reason for justifiable pride and enormous gratification. This sense of pride will, most of all, be felt by those who feel family values strongly, and so interpret this crossing as a duty towards those who have come before and those who will follow. The preoccupations, disagreements, and disappointments that are present in any professional situation can sometimes be more acute and painful if we live them in a family context. I believe, though, that satisfaction can more than compensate; at least, this has been my personal experience.

Going back to a possible answer to the question you are asking each other, or yourselves: "Will I join the business, or not?" "And if I join, is it better to do so at the beginning of my work experience or later on?" My suggestion is to allow conditions to mature to the point where you can make a decision with the highest probability of success. So when will that be? When you can say that you know yourselves well, that you know how to judge yourselves, and that you are able to place your aspirations in relation to the context you have in mind.

I think you'll be better able to do this after you've lived through work experiences outside the company for a long enough period of time. This way you'll have acquired the elements of evaluation necessary to verify, with serene objectivity, whether the family business wants you and whether you want it – with equal intensity. Two needs, two sets of requirements, two coherent potentialities must come together, or any "marriage" will be born under an unlucky star.

I realize only now, near the end of my missive, that I haven't given you any practical advice on how to succeed once you've joined the business. Perhaps it's there between the lines. It seemed opportune, first and foremost, to clarify and emphasize how important it is to make the right decision from the start; this is what I've tried to tell you. If you do join the family business, you may have to read more carefully the letters other entrepreneurs have written to their children!

All my love,

Papà

Translated and re-printed from an Italian book entitled "*Lettere al futuro – Il passaggio dell'azienda da una generation all'altra. Le testimonianze di 33 imprenditori di successo*" (Gianfilippo Cuneo, Milano: Baldini&Castoldi s.r.l., 1999). Used with permission of the author of the letter and the publisher.

Paulig Ltd

Location: Helsinki, Finland

Turnover (in US$): $170 million (2000)

Date of exchange rate: July 2001

Name of local currency: Finnish Mark (FIM)

Number of employees: 445 (2000)

Activity/industry sector: Finland's leading company in the coffee and seasoning business.

Geographic spread of the business: Finland, Scandinavia, the Baltic States and Russia.

Year the business was started: 1876

Name of the founder and relation to the author: Gustav Paulig (great grandfather of the author)

Generation running the business: 4th

Name & position of person writing the letter: Bertel Paulig – Executive Chairman.

Other family members active in the business: Eduard Paulig, younger brother of the author.

% of capital owned by the family: 100% owned by 50-60 family member (3rd – 5th generations)

Recipient(s) of the letter: all family members.

Source: Booklet *"125 years of enjoyable moments – Paulig,"* text: Mariitta Hämäläinen, Studio Poema Oy, translation: John Arnold, publisher: Paulig Ltd, Finland, 2001

Bertel Paulig to his family members

Dear family,

The International Paulig Group of today is different from the Paulig of yesterday, and it will
probably be different tomorrow. And yet, in spite
of change – and growth – the fundamental concept of Paulig's business has remained the same
for one-hundred twenty-five years: offer the best
products to meet consumers' needs. Throughout

Bertel Paulig

our history, the Paulig family has made it a trademark to keep an open mind,
anticipate changes and convert them into opportunities. The fuel for progress
has always been fresh business ideas combined with the boldness to make them
happen. The same is still true today: we aim to be a bold pioneer, not pushed
by the past, but drawn by a vision of the future. Continuing success is possible
only if you can anticipate tomorrow's quality requirements today. This means
constantly being on the move with our eyes open and, at the same time, having
the ability and courage to see opportunities where others do not see them.

This is exactly what our founder, Gustav Paulig, did in June 1876 when he
started selling green coffee, spices, loaf sugar, rice, raisins, dried fruit, oils, port
and cognac in his first goods shop. In the first year sales of green coffee reached
303,000 kilos, 7% of Finland's total coffee imports. Here was the first proof that
Gustav, then only twenty six years old, had a unique ability to anticipate change
and turn it into a business opportunity. As his business became more successful, he augmented his wares with rye and wheat flour, American fat and
German lard, and even unusual spices and delicacies. So in 1896, when a new
Finnish cook book made exotic ingredients such as lemon peel, almonds, vanil-
la, parsley, nutmeg, currants, ginger and cayenne pepper popular much in
demand in Finnish households, Gustav Paulig was ready. But innovation did
not stop there. Gustav soon had another successful business idea: easing house-
wives' work by roasting and grinding coffee for them. The product sold so well
that Gustav built up a nation-wide sales network, and as the business grew, so
too did Gustav's reputation for high ethical standards, precision and quality.
He took special care of his staff, every day making them porridge and coffee.
"Your actions and speech," he liked to remind them, "always stand for the
name and the values of the company. When you start compromising on quality, you might as well shut the factory gates."

After Gustav's death in 1907, his wife Bertha, who had been his confidante and
business advisor for more than thirty years, took over the family business. Only
two years later, sensing a pioneering opportunity, she bought three coffee shops

Gustav Paulig   *Bertha Paulig*   *Eduard Paulig*

and popular cafés. The small chain grew to 25 cafés and a bakery, with Paulig's own brand of tea, and soon, Eduard Paulig, one of four Paulig sons and three daughters, returned from his apprenticeship to run the expanding business. Following his father's principles, Eduard travelled widely to forge better ties with the company's suppliers and customers. In 1919 Bertha made the trading house a limited liability company and transferred all the shares to Eduard, who became the managing director of A.B. Gustav Paulig O.Y. Bertha was now able to live out the Paulig sense of social responsibility, giving liberally of her time and energy to those less fortunate, which included co-founding a children's day-care centre known today as the Bertha Maria Home.

By the early 1920s coffee had become a staple of the typical Finnish country breakfast, and Paulig was selling coffee beans in five-, ten- and twenty-kilo bags. But in April 1924 Mathias Eriksson, a shopkeeper from Finland's Åland province, sent Eduard Paulig a postcard gently urging the company to pack coffee in 250- and 500-gram packs for consumers. Seeing the potential of Eriksson's novel idea, Eduard immediately carried it out. And a few years later, he travelled to the coffee-growing regions of South and Central America to make vital personal connections that would fuel the company's success for decades. Over the years, Eduard "kept his eyes open," responding to market changes by dropping sugar, flour and salt, adding dried fruit, canned foods, cheese and caviar, and introducing special jars to preserve the flavours of Paulig seasonings. Further innovations included ready-ground coffee and the date-stamping of coffee packages (Paulig was the first in Europe to do so). During the years of the Great Depression, Paulig's original coffee substitute (a blend with 15% real coffee) became so popular that the company continued making it long after the economy improved.

The World War II years were a major challenge for Paulig, but the company responded – yet again – with a number of innovations. When food rationing was introduced in Finland and coffee was confiscated at the end of October 1939, Paulig produced its second coffee substitute, this time with 25% real coffee. In December 1941 coffee was distributed for the last time, so Paulig started selling a 100% rye and barley substitute. Later that year, Paulig was forced to close its office in Tallinn (Estonia), a set-back the company would make up for only years later. During the war years the armed forces needed to get fresh meat to the field kitchens, so they turned to Henrik Paulig, Eduard's eldest son, who had learned about a new preservation technique during a study trip to America: deep freezing. On leave from his front-line duties, he bought the needed refrigeration equipment in Europe and, in 1942, the first frozen-food plant in the Nordic region began delivering to the army. Through all the ups and downs of the Great Depression and the five years of war, Eduard Paulig never wavered in his belief in the importance of people, and that the company had "the best employees": he paid full wages to those away on military service, and every employee received a gift box at Christmas, Easter and the Midsummer holiday.

Finnish civilians tasted their first deep frozen food in the 1940s – peas, loganberries and crayfish — and Paulig seized the opportunity to offer frozen Baltic herrings, frozen ready-made meals and ice-cream. The next generation became even more active in the company in the 1950s when Torsten, Eduard's second son, became the editor-in-chief of Paulig's staff magazine and Henrik took over from his father, becoming the company's new managing director. At the time, all five of Eduard's children received equal shares of the business. By now, coffee had become the drink of choice for Finnish adults and children alike, a trend that Paulig turned to advantage by printing pictures of cars and other motor vehicles on its rigid carton coffee packages (a total of 216 collectable pictures) . The 216 collectible car cards started a craze among children and drove considerable market growth. The Paulig family council was established and started a tradition of family members gathering three times a year to learn about the business, taxation, coffee, ethics and many other topics.

In the next decades, Paulig focused exclusively on food production and then expanded into shipping which, by the end of the 1970s, became a third division alongside coffee and frozen foods. Paulig started the Coffee Institute in 1980, the second food-service training institute of its kind in the world. American Jubilee products joined Paulig's range in 1983, with the now-familiar hot-chocolate machines in petrol stations around Finland, and then came Tazza

Exterior of Paulig Ltd.

Coffee tasting in the mid-1960's: Börje Uunila (left), Henrik Paulig, Gunnar Winqvist and Kurt Richter.

and Vaseco, a company specialised food and beverage vending machines for the workplace. In 1982, Henrik died unexpectedly in his mid-60s, and I became the chief executive. Back then, we had no succession plans, a lack we set out to correct immediately, and now, twenty years later, a very good succession plan is in place. During their school years all family members are encouraged to take summer jobs at Paulig. We welcome every member of the family in the business provided, of course, they satisfy market criteria. Before they can join us, however, they need to work for at least ten years outside the family business, and even then they have to compete with outsiders. We try to have more than one family member working in the business at the same time.

In 1986, still aiming to be a pioneer company, Paulig acquired a majority shareholding in Appleton, Machin & Smiles Ltd, a London-based coffee firm, and thus began an international expansion that continued with the acquisition of Britain's best-known brand of roast ground coffee, Lyons, which incidentally, we sold at the end of the decade. We streamlined our operations, sold off our frozen food interests, leaving coffee, hot beverages and seasonings as our core competencies, and set-up a new spice division (1987). The market for snacks was growing, so we founded our successful joint venture with the Scandinavian enterprise Estrella. In the early 1990s, we formed the Nordic Spice Alliance with Nordfalks AB of Sweden and Danski Krydderier A/S of Denmark in order to expand further by collaborating on purchasing, production, product development and marketing. Soon, our Santa Maria seasonings could be found in the kitchens of the Baltic States, Russia and continental Europe. And finally, after a fifty year wait, we were among the first to reopen business relationships with our old trading partners in Estonia. This is no coincidence, for I believe that we have a moral duty to aid and assist in rebuilding the Baltic States. But I also see our social responsibility extending to the environment, which is why we have tried to develop more environmentally friendly packaging solutions and production methods. Paulig upgraded its packaging machinery and was the first in Finland to launch a handy, simple laminate package that produces less waste. For the international market, we are also pursuing new solutions for functional foods, and we are patenting Diminicol®, an ingredient that reduces cholesterol.

What does all this history teach us? Gustav Paulig, the founder of our family business, saw the opportunities of tomorrow before others. He built his company on ethical responsibility, quality, uncompromising professionalism and honest partnership. This strong foundation has lasted through thick and thin, from generation to generation, for 125 years. I sincerely hope that our generations, the 4th and 5th, will build on the past to be tomorrow's pioneers. I hope we will look for and find new opportunities while remaining true to Gustav Paulig's values. I count on you to embrace this challenge for our generation and the next, and to instil these values in your children so that the legacy of Gustav Paulig will remain vivid for a long, long time.

Bertel

Bertel Paulig

Executive Chairman

Paulig Group

Finland

Algar Grupo

Location: Uberlandia, MG, Brazil

Turnover (in US$): $600 million

Date of exchange rate: September 26, 2001

Name of local currency: Reais

Number of employees: 6,500

Activity/industry sector: Telecommunications; Agribusiness.

Geographic spread of the business: Brazil Central.

Year the business was started: 1907

Name of the founder and relation to the author: Jose & Alexandrino Garcia.

Generation running the business: 4th

Name & position of person writing the letter: Luiz Alberto Garcia, Chairman.

Other family members active in the business: Luiz Alexandre Garcia, Co Chairman.

Other family members non-active shareholders: none.

% of capital owned by the family: >70%

Recipient(s) of the letter: Children of the author: Ana Marta & Luiz Alexandre Garcia; Grandchildren of the author: Rayza Garcia Carvalho, Sanyla Garcia Carvalho, Caio Augusto Garcia and Tassio Alexandre Garcia and grandchildren to come.

Source: Letter of Recommendations from the ALGAR 2100 convention, dated March 2000, at "Pousada do Rio Quente Resorts."

Luiz Alberto Garcia to his children and grandchildren

Carta meus filhos,

To my children, my grandchildren and their descendants:

The Algar Group had its origins far away from here, much farther away than anyone can imagine, in a small village in the northern region of Portugal where my grandparents, Josefina and José Alves Garcia, once lived. Way back, at the beginning of the 20th century, they had the idea of seeking new opportunities, and so they immigrated to Brazil. Over three generations, through great persistence, hard work and faith we are still very proud of today, my grandparents, my uncles, my father and my siblings built a model enterprise. My father, Alexandrino Garcia, led a special team of dedicated and qualified co-workers that helped him lead our Group to success.

I write to you today as a member of the fourth generation, Chairman of our Board of Directors, working to perpetuate our enterprise and keep expanding its growth opportunities. As Chairman, I am in a position to see the whole of the forest, not just one tree, as so often happens when one is inside the forest or, in the case of running a business, preoccupied with details. In my early days in the business, perhaps I saw only the tree. I used to think, as my grandfather and my father did, that "I do the best I can, and after my time, the problems will be yours." But now, from my wider perspective, I have changed my mind. Today I am convinced I have an obligation to offer you some tools you can use whenever you need, at will.

Of these tools, it now seems to me, the most important are our Algar Group Beliefs & Values and our Management Principles, for they are immutable.

Beliefs & Values	Management Principles
Human Talents	Team Spirit
Transparency	Commitment
Return to Our Investors	Human and Professional Growth
Entrepreneurial Spirit	Educative Leadership
Permanent Change	Responsible Freedom of Action
Enchantment of the Client	Participation in the Decision-Making Process
Social Responsibility	
Our Corporate Brand	Acknowledgement of Different Levels of Responsiblity
Our Business Reputation	
Brazil	"Associate" instead of Employee

With these beliefs, values and principles, we shall always have an orientation. For they give us the right guidance to shape our business principles and properly direct our actions and our conduct. They are, in my view, the best legacy for the perpetuity of our Group.

Another very valuable tool is Algar 2100, since it compels us to think 100 years ahead. It serves, therefore, as a fresh source of renewable attention to and high regard for the future. The Board of Directors is also of the greatest importance, because it is where our family holds half of the seats and where the other half is occupied by the best professionals of the highest qualifications and principles. All of us, together, hold the autonomous responsibility for deciding the future of the Algar Group.

It also seems to me that if you, as family members, wish to work to perpetuate the family enterprise, you should especially honor the article of the Family Constitution that requires all members of the family who wish to hold a job in the Group first to hold a job for two years outside Algar – and earn a good record, too.

I trust that our Algar Group will thrust itself successfully into the future if we preserve, enjoy and practice these valuable guidelines, electing the road of truth, justice and goodness, under the light of God.

Luiz Alberto Garcia

President

Algar Group

Brazil

4

WOMEN IN
FAMILY BUSINESSES

Traditionally, women at the top of family firms are only daughters who
have taken over from their fathers, such as Antonia Ax:son Johnson (Sweden)
who successfully runs Axel Johnson AB, one of the largest privately-owned
businesses in Europe; or they are widows who, when their husbands die, take
up the reins of the business, either because they have already been involved a
long time, or because their children are too young to take over. Ardath Rodale,
whose letter follows in this chapter, exemplifies the widow who inherits the
family business and becomes a successful family-business chairwoman in her
own right. Another well-known example is Katharine Graham of The
Washington Post Company (USA).

More and more, however, as the Al-Khonaini (Kuwait) letter in this
chapter illustrates, business owners are offering their daughters top job opportunities. A Mass Mutual survey of family businesses in the USA indicated that,
among New York respondents, 30% said their next chief executive would likely be a woman.[5] One reason for this change is probably the fact that more and
more often, daughters now receive the same education as sons. They go to top
schools and are often eager to prove themselves, which motivates them to succeed in business careers.

In addition, women are often good ambassadors for the business and are
keen to pursue the family mission. They tend to favor relationships and harmony among people. According to Korman and Hubler (1988) women are
good communicators and have traditionally been more compliant and less
independent than men, who have been more competitive and task-oriented.
Kets de Vries (1996) also suggests that succession from a father to his daughter

– or from a mother to her son – is usually smoother and less strongly marked by conflict than from a father to a son who may actually compete for the leadership position. All of these findings and the trends we have observed suggest that, given the chance, women can prove very valuable as leaders of the family firm.

⁵Cited from *Crain's New York Business*, September 29, 1997, Crain Communications Inc., U.S.A., 1997.

Al Khonaini Al Katami Trading & Contracting Co.

Location: Shuwaikh Industrial Area - Kuwait

Turnover (in US$): $12,400,000

Date of exchange rate: December 23, 2001

Name of local currency: Kuwaiti Dinars

Number of employees: 130-140

Activity/industry sector: Dealers in office & domestic furniture, decoration, electrical & fire-fighting equipment, machinery & special building materials, sino projects, spare parts & workshop.

Year the business was started: 1953

Name of the founder and relation to the author: Mr. Mohammed Abdullah Al Khonaini, father of the author.

Generation running the business: 2nd

Name & position of person writing the letter: Mona Al Khonaini, Chairperson & Department Head for home furniture.

Other family members active in the business: Ghassan (brother), General Manager & Board member; Shaikha (sister), Board member; Munzer (brother), Assistant Manager for Special Building Materials Department; Nizar (brother), Assistant Manager for Decoration Department.

Other family members non-active shareholders: 2 sisters: Haifa and Wafa,

Percentage of capital owned by the family: 100%

Recipients of the letter: Siblings of the author: Shaikha, Haifa, Ghassan, Munzer, Nizar & Wafa.

Mona Al Khonaini to her siblings

My Dear Sisters and Brothers,

We meet every weekend for lunch or dinner. We speak to each other and share our problems and happiness. But deep in my heart, I have one specific thing I cannot leave for our weekly meetings: my love for my sister and brother. I am writing to tell you I care for you all a lot.

I love you above all things, and I will love you till the last breath of my life.

Being the eldest among you, I will try to do my best for you all, according to the wisdom and knowledge I gained from our father, Mohammed Abdullah Al Khonaini. Our father, may god bless his soul, was not only a great father. He was a wonderful guide, a loving and true friend. He was very close to me, and we used to sit and talk for hours. Our mother, may god bless her soul, was a sweet lady. Though she did not indulge much in business matters, I can say, "she had the qualities of a strong lady behind every successful man." She always gave me her full support and co-operation in every walk of my life.

Foreigners often ask me how a woman can run a business in the Middle East. My first answer is this: women in business, especially in the Middle East, have the same rights as men. It is not difficult for a lady to be a leading business woman if she has full confidence and spirit. In the Middle East, although rules and regulations may change from place to place, in general, a woman has, by law and the dictates of religion, the same rights as a man. My second answer is more personal: father and mother's support helped me through it. From the very beginning, my father asked me to accompany him to all meetings, conferences, exhibitions, and fairs, whether they were business, commercial or social. In all places, he put me in front of the guests or friends and introduced me as "Mona, my business partner" rather than "Mona, my eldest daughter." My father's deference and respect inspired in me a great desire to continue his dreams of establishing a well-recognised company and making them come true. Since the first day of my stepping into the business world, I found no difficulty in communicating or dealing with people. Wherever I went, whether it was government offices, banks, companies or clients, I found respect. This gave me a good push. I also had help from the many Kuwaiti friends who knew my father from business circles: they congratulated me for my firm step into the field of business and for my success. Today, Al Khonaini Al Katami is a leading company in the Kuwait business world, and one of the best known.

Father started in 1953 as the sole owner of a single trading company that sold mainly products such as machinery and generators on commission. Three years later, to expand the business, he started a joint venture with Mr. Qatami, a cousin of our mother. Over the years, the business has widened and grown, but it still remains essentially the same business. Today, we employ 130 to 140 staff who work at the administrative level, clerical level, sales levels, as well as site staff and labourers. Nothing specific has changed, but we have improved a lot and added two non-family members to our Board of Directors. Each department – office furniture, domestic furniture, decoration, electrical, fire-fighting, the Sino project, the workshop for machinery and special building materials – is a full-fledged company, with our products and agencies.

As I've implied, I gained a lot of knowledge and wisdom from my father's positive attitude and approach. His most positive act was his 1979 decision to divide his 50% shares in Al Khonaini Al Katami Trading and Contracting Co. into 10 equal shares for his wife and children, including himself, equally, regardless of sex or status (married or not). This was something new, something that had never taken place during this period, especially in the Arab world and wider Muslim community. According to the rules of Islam, the wife should get one third of the shares, and the sons get double that of the daughters (i.e., if each daughter gets 2 shares, each son gets 4 shares) because, in Islam, the brother is responsible for his family when the parents are deceased. If a problem comes to any female family member, the brother has to take care of her.

In 1980, one year after my father's remarkable act, my brother Abdulla passed away, and his shares were distributed to his legal heirs: father and mother (according to Islamic inheritance law, his legal heirs were the father and mother.) Our father passed away in 1991, immediately after Kuwait's Liberation, and our mother passed away in 1999. My mother's shares were divided among her legal heirs – sons and daughters – according to Islamic rules: her sons received double the number of shares as her daughters did. For the future, we have no written rules about share transfer to the next generation. Upon the death of any shareholder, shares will go to his or her legal heirs according to the Islamic law and religion that we all respect.

Our father, Mohammed Abdulla Al Khonaini, was a man with an open mind and an advanced outlook. His life was a clear and open book. He always did what he thought was right and what his conscience said was correct. As such, he made the division of the shares very early, so that all his family members got their equal shares and rights, and so that the company would continue smoothly, even after his death.

We are now in the new era, 2001, stepping forward into the wonderful future ahead of us. We are a very strong family. We have done our level best to honour our father's name, and now we can proudly say that his hard efforts were not in vain. He started the company we know today as a partnership, and today we all stand united: we have acquired the other 50% shares from our partners, and, at present, Al Khonaini family members own it outright.

My heart feels very light as I write this letter to you. Maybe I would not have been able to tell you my sentiments over one of our weekend conversations, but now am sure that they will reach you one day. You will always keep me in your sweet memory as a loving sister who made things happen to help us remain united. My only aim and message to you all is this: let's love each other always and remain united. 'Unity is strength. United we remain forever as divided we may fall'. This message of love and relationship I would also like to pass on to my brothers- and sisters-in-law as well as my dearest nephews and nieces.

Dear brothers and sisters, you will take over the business after me and brother Ghassan Al Khonaini, and your children will be the third generation for Al Khonaini Al Katami Co. Let's do our best to remain united forever.

I will keep loving you all my life,

Mona

PS - This letter was written on Monday, November 19, 2001. It was nine in the morning and I was in the office. The weather was very bad, very dusty and windy. I was very sick and was just sitting on my chair to relax a little. I just closed my eyes for a minute and my memories took me back 45 years.

Rodale Inc.

Location: Emmaus, PA, USA

Number of employees: 1,000

Activity/industry sector: Publishing books & magazines

Geographic spread of the business: Worldwide

Year the business was started: 1930

Name of the founder and relation to the author: J. I. Rodale, Father-in-Law

Generation running the business: Second & third

Name & position of person writing the letter: Ardath Rodale, Chairman, 2nd generation

Other family members active in the business: 4 siblings of the 3rd generation

Other family members non-active in the business: 10 members of the 4th generation

% of capital owned by the family: 100%

Recipient(s) of the letter: 4 members of the 3rd generation

Ardath Rodale to her family

To My Dear Family,

I am so proud that we are a family-owned business! We are free to decide how we want to grow. I know that as long as we move forward, being cheerleaders to help each one be the best we can be, and reach out with understanding and love, we will be winners.

It is hard to project what the company will be like in twenty years. I hope and dream that the family will be strongly unified. As we look at the world today, it is so vitally important to make a difference for peace and health in our environment at home and throughout the world. At Rodale we do our part by publishing magazines and books. Our mission *to inspire and enable people to improve their lives and the world around them* is expanding worldwide.

I married Bob when he had just turned 21, and I was 22. When he asked me to marry him, I said to myself, "Not only do I marry you, but I also marry the mission of the family and the company." I believed the dream!

My father-in-law, J. I. Rodale, was very innovative and intuitive. He started the business in 1940 by publishing *Organic Gardening* magazine. The emphasis was on healthy soil and healthy people. He was the first person to coin the word "organic." As J.I. read the readers' letters, he discovered that more and more subscribers were deeply frustrated with answers to their health problems from the medical establishment. One day, he came into the office he shared with Bob and described his new venture, *Prevention* Magazine – a periodical aimed at preventing disease instead of looking for a cure. Bob looked at his father and said, "Holy cow, that's a bad idea." J.I. never took no for an answer. He said to Bob, "OK. You do *Organic Gardening*, and I'll do *Prevention*." An advertisement went out inviting subscriptions, and the magazine was an immediate success.

J.I. was one of those rare people blessed with far-reaching vision. In his mind, he could climb a high mountain and see the world far into the future. He held no fear for sharing his beliefs and his ideas for better health. He was a tribal leader who valued the land and its people. He believed that the world and all those who inhabit it have a legacy to pass on to the generations that follow. He believed people could grow healthier by eating food grown in healthy soil.

J.I. had little yellow pads way before Post-it Notes were invented. He was constantly writing down his ideas for the magazines and many of his other myriad interests. On any given day, you could see him driving down the road or walking the fields while writing these notes. Our archive building is filled with shoeboxes of notes filed by subject, such as sleep disorder, overweight people, cancer, fluoridation, etc. He was always looking toward the next horizon.

Bob's contribution to *Prevention* was bringing credibility to his father's ideas. He sought out researchers who could prove some of his theories. Bob was the one to carry through his father's ideas. He was also an intuitive, creative person but was more methodical. He felt that running the company each day was not the best use of his time, so he asked me what I thought and suggested another loyal person in the company be appointed Chief Operating Officer.

Bob was interested in spreading the mission not only in the United States but worldwide. He worked with farmers and agricultural experts, the U.S. Department of Agriculture, and other leaders throughout the world. Tragically, he was killed in Russia in 1990 while trying to start a magazine for the Russian people on gardening and health. He was very excited about how things were going. While traveling to the airport in a van on his way home, he, his Russian counterpart, their interpreter, and the van driver were all killed when they were hit by a city bus. It was a devastating blow for all of us.

I had begun working for the company after I had three children. We were going to start construction on our very first building, and I wanted to have the job of working with the architect and doing all the decoration. We have an extensive art collection, and part of the fun of that work would be trying to make an office environment feel like home! I told Bob that I really wanted that job for my own. He agreed, and I gave him a paper and pen and said, "Write down that I can have the job for as long as I want." When he'd done that, I said, "Now we will attach the company seal, and I will put this in the safety deposit box." That's where it is still to this day!

Today, all of you surviving children and I are shareholders. I wish David were alive to be part of this group. His death from AIDS in 1985 hurt us all very deeply. Among his many talents, he was a whiz at electronics. He is still in our hearts. While I have the majority of the company's stock, in future the stock will be divided equally. If there is a tie vote, Maria, who will succeed me as Chairperson, will cast the tiebreaker.

My family has always come first; the company was second. I worked hard to make sure that you would grow up in the right way. I went to bat many times for things you wanted to do. I hope I have succeeded. I am so very proud of all four of you and your many accomplishments.

Anthony, as Chairman of the Rodale Institute, your work and strong commitment to helping people around the world create a regenerative food system that renews environmental and human health have inspired all of us. Your program aims to find agricultural solutions to hunger, malnutrition, disease, and soil degradation. We believe healthy soil makes healthy food and healthy people and affects each one of us – our children, the community, the nation, and the world. I am proud of Florence, your wife, for her outstanding contribution to the Institute's programs for children world-wide, including the marvelous website, www.kidsregen.org.

Heather, you have done a fantastic job as Vice President of Leadership Development in our Human Resources department. I am touched by how you share your heart and care for all those people who come to you for help. You have brought a high level of quality and expertise to the training and development programs we offer our employees. Your commitment to life-long learning motivates others toward excellence. Your help has made our child care center an outstanding place for children to learn and grow. I also want to thank your husband, Tom, for his years of dedication to our company and its mission.

Heidi, I am proud of the high quality magazine, *Fitness Swimmer*, which you were instrumental in creating. Although we weren't able to pick up as many advertisers and subscriptions as we had hoped, the magazine had a great impact on the swimming world, especially during the 2000 Olympics when you supervised the exciting website which kept fans throughout the world tuned in to the latest swimming results during the games. You made great contacts with people internationally during your travels for the magazine and book division, and that experience will benefit you and our company as we develop new business opportunities.

Maria, I am very proud of all the fine work you have been doing as Vice Chairman to help our company move ahead. I am grateful for the way you have helped to make all the new executives feel welcome and for listening to their ideas for moving forward in a positive way. Your brainchild, our magazine *Organic Style*, is gorgeous and informative, and we are all cheering it on to success. I am also proud of your husband, Lou Cinquino, for his bright mind and caring nature; he has made a tremendous contribution to our book division.

The company was always part of your lives growing up. We had exciting times, great trips, and met exciting people. You were all exposed to a wide variety of experiences that many of your peers didn't have. Did you ever sit down to make a list of all the things you were thankful for in your lives? I've made mine, and it is overwhelming. I am so happy to be alive.

Now, for the first time in the history of our company, there is a non-family Chief Executive Officer. Steve Murphy has been with us now for two years. He loves the company and is working very hard. Steve brought in fantastic new people with high energy and new ideas. It was during this exciting yet stressful period of change that I got cancer for the third time. I am using alternative healing, and I feel good. My energy level has never gone down.

I think we are evolving in the right direction with the Board of Directors. In addition to the five of us, Steve and our financial officer are voting members. A lawyer and consultant are non-voting members. We are looking to add two outside members as well. At some stage, we hope some of the grandchildren will step forward with new vision to take part in this great venture we have begun.

While we might not see each other every day, we have shareholders meetings once a week. Recently, we discovered that we sometimes mix shareholders and family issues. We must learn to separate them. When Bob was alive, we had dinners once a week. Now, as the grandchildren grow up, we get together less often. The last time was Thanksgiving. I hope that we have more time for the grandchildren, for they are the ones I am concerned about. You, my children, were all so close to the company and each other growing up. Now, we live ten minutes from each other, but the grandchildren have scattered across the country. Sarah, Shelbi, Maya, Marlow, Gillian, Alex, Geoff, Andrew, Coco, and Eve are a wonderful bunch of grandchildren, and it looks as if they are all creatively inclined.

Recently I found a paper I had written a while back, and the message still is very real. I asked three important questions:

What is my dream? It is for a world of peace, prosperity for the company and the Institute, and for each of these enterprises to be world giants.

What about Ardie? I want to reach out to others, love my children and grandchildren with a passion, and I want for all of them to find happiness within themselves to be successful and understand each other as they reach out to touch other people's lives with love.

What do I want for Ardie? I hope for love, appreciation, honor, and respect. Don't take away my power to be!

If I have one last message to you, my grandchildren, it would be this: the most important thing we share as a family is that we work together. Communicate your wonderful ideas as we interact with one another. Reach out and realize all the great opportunities there are to make a difference in the world. Even if you don't work for Rodale, have a mission to make the world a better place. Reach out to be kind and understanding. You will have a fantastic legacy. Regardless of what you choose to do, you must have compassion and understanding to rise above prejudice. Sometimes that comes through learning from hard experiences.

On J.I.'s and Bob's tombstone this message is inscribed: "He urged man to live in harmony with the world."

To do that creates a magnificent masterpiece for life!

My deepest love to each one of you!

Mom, Ardie, Ummy

5

SHARED LEADERSHIP

By definition, shared leadership is when, instead of the usual one person, two or more people assume the chief executive position of a family company. Over the past decade, the model has gained considerable popularity in the USA, possibly because family members at the siblings or cousins stage typically receive a high level of education, so that several are competent to take on the CEO role. The practice of shared leadership started much earlier in Europe than in the USA – its roots stretch deep into the 19th century – which may explain why cases of shared leadership seem to be more frequent in Europe than in the USA.

What is the key difficulty in shared leadership? Sharing authority – having to compromise on the ego side. A shared leadership position holds less glamour, and may thus be less attractive to potential successors. However, if co-leaders respect each other, if their strengths are complementary and they build on them, and if their commitment to the business and the family outstrips their personal ambition, shared leadership can prove very successful. Puig Corp., in Spain,[6] is a prime illustration. As noted earlier, four siblings of the second generation worked as a team at the top for forty-five years. They knew that, together, they could bring more strength and resources to the company. The formula worked for them, and they handed over the management to another team of four, three from the third generation and a manager from outside the family.

This chapter's letter from Dr. Peter Zinkann shows how shared leadership has been advantageous for Miele, the German family company, and has avoided many mistakes. Rudolf Miele and Peter Zinkann, third generation, tell us that relinquishing some authority and sharing the Miele leadership was not difficult – two generations of predecessors had done the same. Their grandfathers, Carl Miele and Reinhard Zinkann, had founded the business, and run it successfully under the flag of shared leadership. The third generation, Rudolf Miele and Peter Zinkann, knew from early childhood that they would either have to share the Miele leadership or work outside. Both of them happily opted to share the leadership. Recently they passed the scepter of the family business to the fourth generation of shared leadership: Reinhard Zinkann and Markus Miele.

[6]FBN Conference Paris, 1998. Ogunsdulire M. (2001).

Miele & Cie GmbH

Location: Gütersloh, Germany

Turnover (in US$): $2 billion (2000)

Date of exchange rate: September 2001

Name of local currency: Deutsch Mark (German Mark)

Number of employees: 15,000

Activity/industry sector: Manufacturer of high-end domestic appliances.

Geographic spread of the business: 60 % of sales outside Germany (1999) – Europe, USA, Canada, South Africa, Australia, Japan and Hongkong through own subsidiaries, other markets through authorised importers.

Year the business was started: 1899

Name of the founder and relation to the author: Carl Miele and Reinhard Zinkann (grand-father of the author)

Generations of both families running the business: 3rd and 4th

Name & position of person writing the letter: Dr Peter Zinkann, 3rd generation, co-managing director

Other family members active in the business: 3rd generation Rudolf Miele, Gerhard Miele – 4th generation Dr. Markus Miele, Dr. Reinhard Zinkann

Other family members non-active shareholders: 60 members of the second to fifth generation.

% of capital owned by the families: 100%

Recipient(s) of the letter: Dr. Markus Miele, Dr. Reinhard Zinkann

Sources:
1. Dr Peter Zinkann's speech in Berlin on October 20, 2000 upon receipt of the "German Marketing Prize 2000"
2. May P., Sieger G., & Rieder G. (1999). *Familienunternehmen heute – Jahrbuch 2000*. Bonn, Germany: Intes Akademie für Familienunternehmen

Carl Miele
1869 - 1938

Reinhard Zinkann
1869 - 1939

Carl Miele
1897 - 1986

Kurt Christian Zinkann
1904 - 1985

Rudolf Miele
1929

Dr. Peter Zinkann
1928

Dr. Markus Miele
1968

Dr. Reinhard Zinkann
1959

Dr Peter Zinkann to Reinhard Zinkann and Markus Miele

Dear Reinhard, Dear Markus,

Naturally, I am pleased that you are following in Rudolf Miele's and my foot-steps. But try not to do so by stepping into our shoes! Times change: new questions arise and need to be addressed in new ways. Just as I had to find new solutions over the years, you will have to seek new solutions for today and tomorrow. In your future in Miele, only two things are likely to remain the same. First, any business needs to have a competitive advantage. Be different from your competitors in at least one major way. Bruce Henderson, the founder of Boston Consulting, made this idea part of his credo: "Without a competitive advantage, there is no reason for being in business." And second, being at the head of a family business gives you a clear advantage. You do not have to report to analysts and stock markets every quarter. You do not have to explain to analysts why your performance in this quarter does not meet their expectations. You have the freedom to think in the long run, have visions and be different from generally accepted wisdom.

As I said, you will have to find new solutions for new questions, but still it cannot be wrong for you to try to understand what we did in the past, and why. I believe that as a business we were always very different from other businesses. Over the years, Rudolf Miele and I have done a number of things that were contrary to the generally accepted business wisdom of the time. It was only by being different that we managed to grow a successful business over a century while maintaining it as a 100% family-owned operation that was always free of debt. In the 60s and 70s, when diversification was perceived as the right way to avoid risk, we decided to sell our bicycle and motor-cycle division as well as our agricultural division to concentrate our efforts solely on household appliances. Today this is called focus; at that time, however, the word *focus* was only used for cameras! In those days, it was also common to think that a good manager could manage anything. Rudolf and I were of a different opinion. We believed that love of the product is essential for success in any business. But who can love products as diverse as, say, cheese, underwear, furniture and PCs? You mange best and succeed with what you love. And happy love develops best in monogamy, so to speak. That sounds old fashioned, I know, but we believe it.

After the heyday of focus came the time when cold, tough management was believed to be the only key to success. Everything had to be aligned in terms of cost cutting and cold rationale. It was a time of restructuring and downsizing. In many businesses people were laid off. But not at Miele. At Miele we always believed that quality and humanity belong together. Our employees often remark how, even in times of great insecurity, they always felt at home and secure with us, and how they found a sense of purpose in working for our company. Perhaps this explains why we have always had low employee turnover.

Rudolf and I also believe in a human touch in our business. It is, after all, mutual trust that has made Miele the best-selling brand in the electric retail trade in Europe. We privilege long-term relationships with people and companies who work with us and contribute to our image. Over 90% of Miele's major appliances are sold through specialist dealers with long-term Miele relationships, and we cherish those relationships. Long term cooperation with specialist dealers, for example, offers first-class specialist advice coupled with excellent product displays, and reliable pre- and after-sales service. It also gives dealers the chance to make a name for themselves. We are delighted that there are still some family-run dealerships in Germany whose relationships with Miele date back to the company's founding in 1899.

Our difference from other businesses is also illustrated by our identification with our home country, Germany. Clearly, there are lots of countries where we could produce less expensive home appliances, in some places considerably less expensive. Yet, with its unique geographic location Germany offers a first-class logistic advantage: 70% of Europe's purchasing power is conveniently situated within a 24-hour delivery distance. Moreover, staying close to our roots also means that we have access to a motivated, well-educated, stable workforce. This has a significant impact on the technical reliability of our production processes and prevents mistakes. It is a guarantee of quality.

In addition, in 100 years Miele has only had two generational changes at the top – from the two founders to the second and then to the third generation. This low turnover contradicts not only the current wisdom that "a new broom sweeps clean" but also the belief that in the long-run a two-headed management cannot function well. We have demonstrated the opposite. When the two people who jointly lead the business have a lot of mutual respect and have been brought up knowing that there would be no other path to success, power games are dropped fairly quickly, and the double management can prove very successful. When two people share the management tasks, each has to convince the other of his ideas, arguments and explanations. At Miele, our two-person has lead all along to a healthy constraint that prevented each of us from making some strategic mistakes we probably would have made if we had been on our own.

Rudolf and I also differed from the common wisdom in our views of growth. Naturally, we know that if the business does not grow it will die, but we also believe that a family business cannot grow faster than its shareholders' equity; if it does, it will one day lose its independence. So we have adopted the rule that "we want to grow, but not faster than we could without needing either the capital markets or bank credits".

The most distinctive difference between Miele and our competitors, however, has to do with our brand. All other large companies in our industry sector grow by other acquiring other companies and continuing the production and distribution of the acquired brands. The very large market players manage 15 to 20 brands simultaneously with the intention of reaching as wide a market as possible. At Miele, we think differently. We believe in a unique brand image that serves a specific market, and our belief runs contrary to current marketing theories. We are the only large international company in our field that operates this way, but it works for us.

Miele's success cannot be attributed solely to marketing efforts and senior management; it is the success of the *whole* company. A unique brand image can be maintained only if there is complete accord among the corporate image, the reality of the product, brand communication through advertising and sales personnel, everyday activities and the conviction of the entire workforce, from senior management to staff in labs, production and services. So, what really matters is not merely being different, but rather being *coherent* in the ways we differ. Everything must fit together like the notes in a beautiful piece of music. A single false note in a Mozart string quartet would destroy the overall harmony. The genius of Mozart's music is all the elements fit together perfectly. Naturally, we know all too well that we have yet to reach that perfect Mozart harmony. Far from it. We know that to make our "Forever Better" philosophy come true, a lot of work still needs to be done – more than enough for the next generation!

What is the essence of Miele? At first glance it is quality – our credo that quality comes first, and everything else comes second. At second glance I believe the essence of Miele is love. Not only Rudolf Miele's love and my love for the company, but also the love that the vast majority of our employees bring to their work and to Miele. A Chinese proverb says "If you want to be happy for one hour go to sleep, if you want to be happy for one day go fishing, if you want to be happy for one week slaughter a pig, but if you want to be happy all your life choose a job you love". We both love our work at Miele; it has made both of us happy. This is true not only for us, but also for many of our 15,000 employees. And we hope that our successors and our thousands of employees will also feel at home at Miele and that Miele will make them happy throughout their lives.

Peter

Dr. Peter Zinkann

co-managing director

Miele & Cie. GmbH

Germany

6

WEALTH, TRUSTS AND
STEWARDSHIP

As families grow and advance through the generations, and as business-es grow in complexity and size, new family issues arise. First, as families grow wealthier, parents wonder how to educate their children about the family's affluence. There are, of course, many ways, but general observation suggests that the earlier parents talk to their children about money issues, the better off the children will be in the long run. Not least, parents need to help their children understand that neither the business nor the wealth are guaranteed to last forever. They must put special emphasis on family values. It is also important for them to teach their children to be entrepreneurial, and to get involved in philanthropy and give. Parents need to be aware that inherited wealth can be a burden; not all prospective inheritors feel comfortable with it. By teaching their children at an early age how to handle wealth, parents might well be offering them the best chance at responsible, balanced adulthood.

Second, when a large number of shares are at stake, they are often not transmitted directly to the next generation. Instead they are held in trusts, foundations and/or complex financial entities. These intermediary structures can make successors feel disconnected from the business. The letter by Steven Waichler of Follett in this chapter captures the difficulties faced by families who want to build a spirit of capital stewardship and a legacy for the genera-tions to come.

Third, at this large and complex stage, the distance between family and business and the distance among family members has often widened consider-ably from the early days of rather tight proximity. Since most family members are not active in the business and may live farther apart than ever, they see one another less often than ever before. When families are very large, individual family members are less likely to know one another well. At some meetings of widely dispersed families, members actually wear tags that identify them by name and family branch. Given these realities, parents often wonder, "How do we foster family spirit in such cases?" "How do we pass on passion for the business and commitment to its long-term success when we have never worked in the business, or have only been involved at the company's board level?" "Is it even important to do these things?"

Our observations lead us to say "yes" in at least two cases. First, when the family history has been closely intertwined with the history of the business, or, and even more important, when the name of the family is also the name of the business. Events at companies like Ford in 2001 or Hewlett-Packard in 2002 in the USA show how much families care about the destiny of the family business. When the business is in danger, it is the family name and the family pride that are at stake. In the case of Ford, the family decided to reoccupy a leadership position in the business. In the Hewlett-Packard case, the family owners did not hesitate to become more visible and fight a difficult battle against management over a fundamental question of strategy.

Committed family shareholders are crucial for the business. More than any other investors, family shareholders may be ready to sacrifice some short-term profitability by investing in the business to increase its long-term value. Their willingness and the commitment it entails is vital in difficult times as well as in periods of expansion.

Follett Corporation

Location: River Grove, IL, USA

Turnover (in US$): Sales for Fiscal 2001: $1.55 billion (2001)

Number of employees: Over 10,000

Activity/industry sector: Education markets, distributor and retailer.

Geographic spread of the business: United States and Canada

Year the business was started: 1873

Name of the founder and relation to the author: Charles Barnes (no relation); C.W. Follett (great-grandfather) began working in the business in 1901 and took over ownership in 1926.

Generation running the business: 4th generation

Name & position of person writing the letter: Steven Waichler, family shareholder involved in family governance.

Other family members active in the business: Many family members are active in management.

Other family members non-active shareholders: About one hundred non-active family shareholders (the number keeps rising).

% of capital owned by the family: 98%

Recipient(s) of the letter: Grace Waichler (daughter of the author)

Notes:
The business was founded in 1873 by Charles M. Barnes in Wheaton, Illinois. Three years later, C.M. Barnes & Company moved to Chicago where the business sold new and used textbooks, stationary and school supplies. Charles W. Follett joined the company in 1901, and acquired controlling interest in 1927. His four sons joined him in the business, and created new ventures in publishing, book wholesaling and college retail bookstores. These various companies continued to grow over the next three decades, and in 1957, they were incorporated jointly as Follett Corporation. The second generation's tenure continued into the 1970s.

In the third generation, family management continued to expand and modernize our businesses. New warehousing facilities and computerized distribution systems supported our growing wholesale businesses. We served schools, school libraries and college bookstores. Aggressive growth in the number of contract-managed college bookstores helped lead a ten-fold increase in sales. All of our businesses became leaders in their market segments. Follett developed modern systems for supporting the business units, particularly in finance, human resources and legal support. Business governance and organization continues to evolve as family management moves into the fourth generation. Our Board of Directors includes four independent directors, and our organizational structure is evolving greater market segment focus to leverage business unit synergies.

Steve Waichler to his daughter Grace

March 19, 2002

Dear Grace,

The dictionary defines a legacy as an inheritance or bequest, or "…something that has come from an ancestor or predecessor or the past." Our business, Follett Corporation, is the legacy of several generations of our family. It has been built by many people, working collectively, for over a century. Ownership is a shared inheritance handed down to us by our ancestors. This bequest is not only of great economic value, but it also holds our common history and gives us the chance to transmit our collective wisdom and remembrance.

I have always felt a profound sense of indebtedness to the family and the business. My ownership interest in Follett gave me an opportunity to build economic freedom by saving and investing. Your great-grandfather, Dwight Follett, gave me this opportunity when he gave me my stock. But I also owe a debt to all those who worked to build the Corporation, and enhance the value of my holding. I feel a profound sense of obligation to transmit this gift myself, if possible, enhanced in value.

Many times, Dwight told me he hoped I would save the income from the stock, not live off it. He hoped it would help me have the big things in life, like a house and a family. He hoped I would ultimately have children and pass this gift on to them. In a handwritten letter dated 5.5.1975, he explained his gift to me:

> Dear Steve,
>
> These are the last of my common shares in the Follett Corporation. They come in part from me and in part through me from your great grandfather, Charles W. Follett. May they add to your wellbeing, security, and ability to help others. May they add to your pride in your family. Someday in the future I hope they will be passed on to the next generation.
>
> With love, D

I have often felt conflicted about owning something so valuable, which I have done nothing to create. Not everyone in the family has these feelings, but I want you to know that it is healthy to be uneasy about wealth. My doubts have helped me understand that the stock is something I hold in trust. Wealth creates privileges, but it also creates responsibilities. Safeguarding the stock's value is of paramount importance, and transmitting it, along with its meaning, is my responsibility. And I cannot fulfill my responsibility without writing to you about the business.

The business itself is a living, breathing enterprise. Many people rely on it for their livelihoods and for its services. It can only thrive if we, as owners, put it first. For one hundred years, each generation has enhanced its value, kept that value in the business, and passed it on, through shared stock ownership, to the next generation. This simple combination of preserving value in the business and sharing ownership rests at the core of our family culture, and it has been essential to creating our substantial growth in economic value.

The people who built the business took a legacy view. It was their unspoken culture of ownership. For many years, ownership and management could sit around one table, and there was no need to articulate an ownership vision or talk about our legacy. The family simply shared the labors and the benefits. Without saying it, they knew that the business came first. They built it, not with an end in sight, but rather by thinking long-term. They adapted and worked hard for generations, creating the Follett Corporation we own today.

The task before our generations is different, but just as challenging. We are a much larger family group and only a few of us work in the Corporation. We conceive of ownership differently. We must root our vision in the values of our past, yet focus on building the business for the future. Our business legacy is not a stone monument: the business must change, and will change. The nature of the family or the business may change in ways that are beyond our influence. As owners, we need to assure that the business remains dynamic and creative. Only through hard work and resourcefulness will our inheritance continue to be enriched, and the story of our success still told.

You may never be directly involved in the business, but I hope you will understand and accept the responsibilities of ownership. Today, many family members reject a legacy view of ownership, preferring to see their stock as a personal investment. For many, the stock is their primary personal asset, tying up most of their net worth. Some family members are more concerned with safeguarding their own financial interests than with safeguarding a collective legacy. We should try to understand and respect this view. There will always be different ideas about what stock ownership means.

Nevertheless, each generation must renew the legacy, or it will pass away. In your generation and beyond, ownership will be widely scattered, and views will be more diverse. Enhancing the economic value of individual ownership interests will be vital to holding the family together. Although the stock must remain a well-performing investment, it must also carry a different value for the family. We must cultivate a collective legacy view of ownership that keeps us committed to long-term investment.

Fortunately, Follett has been a great investment; our historical performance has been exceptional. Not only has our capital appreciated dramatically, but current income has also grown strongly. Further, as a closely held company, our capital appreciation is somewhat sheltered from transfer taxes, which enables greater rates of gifting and estate transfer. Think of Follett as a multi-generation investment, designed to build and transfer wealth, and few investments can compare. That is not to say that Follett has always performed well: some difficult times have called for challenging transitions.

The family has faced a number of "moments of truth," where we thought long and hard about our abilities to make the transitions successfully. In those moments, the family bond kept us from selling our common interest, and helped us through the difficult transitions. Looking back, we all benefited economically from that long-term resolve. In the future, to tide us through other transitions, we will need the same, shared trust and pride. An individual ethic of investment may not be enough; we may well need an ethic of family, too, one of a shared stake held in trust for the long-term. I learned this ethic from your ancestors, and it may be the most important lesson of your legacy. I hope you will come to share it with me.

Even with our differences, the family has remained unified in its desire to own the business and to transmit ownership to the next generation. We have kept value in the business and run it conservatively. The capital we have invested is patient; management is allowed to build shareholder value in the most effective ways, even if this takes time. Holding value collectively also helps preserve it, sheltering it from taxation and speculative loss. I hope your generation can learn these lessons and transmit them.

In the future, not everyone will accept that ongoing ownership is in their personal best interest. Some individuals will decide that they want more diversification of their personal assets, or others may disagree with the direction of the company. To foster ongoing unity, some form of liquidity will probably be necessary. I do not oppose liquidity; still, providing it should not harm the company or inhibit its growth, and it should not have a negative impact on those who hold on to their stock.

At some point, some family members may advocate taking Follett Corporation public. Although public ownership can provide both liquidity and the opportunity to acquire new capital, it also dilutes the value of held ownership. I believe the Company can build shareholder value most effectively by remaining privately held. Public companies have a short-term, market-driven focus. Going public is often attractive to those who want to sell, but disadvantageous to those who wish to hold. Only in rare instances can adding public capital provide an opportunity for growth that outweighs the dilution of held equity; so this step must be assessed very carefully and critically.

Further, planning for inheritance taxes is critical to transmission, and providing liquidity sets a tax value for our stock. Before providing liquidity, we should assess the impact on the existing estate planning of shareholders. Generating liquidity for disinterested shareholders can foster ongoing unity in our ownership group, but it can also disrupt the planning of people who want to keep their stock in the family. We should assure transmission first, and provide for liquidity solutions second.

Estate planning is a critical responsibility of ownership that I hope you will take seriously. The idea may seem strange when you first read this letter; after all, you will be young and just beginning to take "ownership" of your inheritance. Much of your stock will still be held in trust. Having children may be far off, and planning for your heirs may seem abstract and not immediately important – that's OK. This letter is for you to keep and reflect on, and it may gain relevance as you grow older.

With responsible financial planning, we have the opportunity to safeguard the stock. First, I hope that you will never need to sell your stock. Selling the stock can only be justified if the best interests of our immediate family are urgently at stake. Only in the rarest instances would our family's short-term needs outweigh the long-term benefits of holding and transmitting the stock. I hope you share this ethic with me. Another way to safeguard our stock is by insuring ourselves against disasters. Insurance costs money, but it is essential that we insure our health, our home, our autos, and, even sometimes, our lives. If we don't, we put our family's future in jeopardy.

Another important part of planning is preparing for transmission. Estate planning also has costs, but it is always cheaper than paying estate taxes. Often, strategies to minimize the cost of transmission are as essential as providing for those costs. Preserving value in transmission is a responsibility we receive with the gift of ownership, and it is one we must strive to pass on. Responsible financial planning is the ethic of our family: the cost of the gift should be borne by the giver, not by their heirs.

I hope you will not see my legacy view as an absolute. It is neither something to defend or to defeat. Many in the family do not see it as a defining element, but I think it will be a vital part of our culture going forward. Our large family needs to cultivate a collective ownership vision; one which is based on a culture of consensus and a pursuit of the right balance of individual and collective interests. I hope you, and others in your generation, will work toward this goal, and share in the pride and care of our family legacy. To ensure success, we must practice stewardship and continue to focus on the long-term, best interests of the business and future generations.

You may view your inheritance differently from me. One day, I hope you will articulate your own vision and ethic of ownership. A good way to start is to write about what ownership means to you, particularly what you would want your heirs to know about the stock. Times change, of course, and so should our vision, matching the challenges of the future. This letter is part of my "ethical will" to you. Some families keep an ethical will for generations, with one generation adding to a previous generation's words. Feel free to add to this or to pass it along.

Before closing, I would like to share your great grandfather's philosophy of money. Dwight believed that everyone should have "his or her own money." He gave this advice to all of us grandchildren, especially the boys. By giving stock to his grandchildren, Dwight intended to give each of us a measure of financial independence. He felt it was vital to have "independence," even in a family, and especially in a marriage. He felt financial independence was particularly important for women. He made sure his wife, Mildred, had her own money to manage and save and spend for herself.

Your great-grandfather was a very wise man. He understood that dependence can be debilitating to self-esteem, and that financial dependence, in particular, can undermine relationships. But he also knew that financial security is a cornerstone of wellbeing. The wealth we inherit gives us an opportunity to build financial independence for ourselves and others. Dwight hoped our stock would provide us with added security, but he also hoped we would not depend on it. This is an important message, since the life of the business is never guaranteed, and depending solely on its dividends does not build security. Secure wealth is built by saving and investing over time. Much of our personal wealth is tied up in a single asset, so diversifying by investing in other assets is essential to building secure wealth.

Our family has a long history of thrift and investment. For many family members money has always had an intrinsic value, not to be wasted. Many fortunes are quickly squandered by their inheritors. I hope you will appreciate the sacrifices made to accumulate your inherited wealth. Be thrifty and develop an ethic of care and stewardship. Always remember what the money is worth to someone who is struggling financially. Our good fortune confers greater responsibility, not less.

Your great-grandfather, Dwight, wrote about adding to my "wellbeing, security, and ability to help others." These are also the things I wish for you. Your inheritance cannot provide them, though. Money alone will never give you "wellbeing" or "security", but can only aid you in attaining them. These qualities depend upon your self-esteem, which, in turn, derives from a productive life and good relationships. Only you can measure how productive your life is. Fill it with experience and inquiry and work. Help others who are less fortunate, through charity and by volunteering your time. Live with compassion for people and the earth. Pay attention to your health. Give yourself time, and share a full and rich life with others. And above all, remember: love is a gift we give others that enriches ourselves.

After Dwight's funeral, we found this bequest written in his trust:

> To my children and their spouses and to my grandchildren and their spouses and great-grandchildren – all of whom have been a special joy to me and who represent for me the unknown future of my own life and the future of our community, our nation and perhaps the world; to each of them now living I bequeath my own share of the marvelous world around us – the mountain and valley, lake and river, sweet birds singing in the gardens, fruits of nature's harvest in the fall, the sweet odor of fresh cut hay and ripe peaches, the glory of red, gold and turquoise sunsets at Shorewood, the burning at noon on the beach, the physical exhilaration of diving through high breaking waves at the sand bar, the exaltation of spirit as one stands beneath the great trees of Muir or Mariposa or the Olympic Peninsula; the feeling of discovery as an island rises out of the Pacific; the tingle of mystery or the abiding sense of continuity of man as one walks ancient ruins; the enigma of life as one looks up at the stars or holds a new baby. Though I bequeath my share of these beauties and marvels from my own joy in the world, in a sense I cannot do so, for they are sights, sounds, and feelings that each must earn by living with awareness and wonder.

Like Dwight, I can add nothing to this bequest. It is miraculously given to each of us; it is already yours. Dwight and I share this wish for you and for all those who follow us into our "unknown future." May you discover for yourself how to live with joy, with appreciation, with awareness and with wonder.

Love,

Your Dad

7

No Successors

Families who have no family successors to manage the business solve the problem in a variety of ways. Usually, they sell the business. A Dutch family could find no motivated successors in a given generation, and eventually sold its business. A mere one generation later, family members identified a competent, motivated family member, bought the business back and installed the new successor at the head of it. More and more often, our observations suggest, families in business refuse to accept the idea that their only alternative to having no direct successor is selling out. So far as they are concerned, having no immediate successor does not have to mean the end of their role in the business.

When there are no direct successors, family members sometimes hand the business over to their nephews and nieces, or skip one generation by putting competent non-family managers in place until their grandchildren are old enough and competent enough to take over. Some families even make it a rule to alternate family chief executives with non-family chief executives, or to choose the best among them. Alternation seems to work well for these family businesses – family members are challenged to prove their talents and non-family managers are motivated by a real opportunity to make it to the top.

The most frequently-used alternative to selling the business – one that has been gaining significant ground over the last fifteen years – is maintaining family ownership of the business but having non-family members run and govern it. For this option to work well, however, family members must learn to be responsible owners. If family members are not interested and committed owners, they might as well sell the business. But if, on the contrary, they are interested and committed, and stay informed on business issues, they can contribute significantly to the prosperity of the business.

The letter of Mr. Fukuhara of Shiseido in this chapter shows us how a family can remain involved in the family business even with a minority ownership. Mr. Fukuhara has been the third generation family leader of Shiseido for a many years. The board and personnel of the company still regard him as a source of inspiration for the business; he is deeply trusted and respected. Nevertheless, the other family members are well-aware that, although they are owners, they will probably never have a place in Shiseido. A fourth Fukuhara may one day lead the business – the road is not blocked – but it will take a very special person to follow in the footsteps of three exceptional family visionaries.

Shiseido Company Limited

Location: Tokyo, Japan

Turnover (in US$): $5.5 billion (March 2001)

Date of exchange rate: Average 2000 (1 US$ = 107.83 Yen)

Name of local currency: Yen

Number of employees: approx. 24,500 (group total)

Activity/industry sector: Manufacture and sales of cosmetics and related products.

Geographic spread of the business: Operating in 65 countries (exports: 15% of total sales).

Year the business was started: 1872

Name of the founder and relation to the author: Arinobu Fukuhara, grandfather of the author.

Generations of family running the business: 3rd

Name & position of person writing the letter: Yoshibaru Fukuhara, Honorary Chairman.

Other family members active in the business: none.

Other family members non-active shareholders: Yuichi Fukuhara.

% of capital owned by the families: 1%

Yoshiharu Fukuhara to his family members

Dear Generations of Shiseido Members,

I am writing not only to tell my predecessors and the future generations of Shiseido Company Limited members – not exclusively Fukuhara family members – how far I have come and where I am now, but also to pass on the lessons I have learned along the way.

Shiseido has a unique history: before becoming a listed company, it started as a family business drugstore that sold prescription medicine; now it is a world-famous cosmetic company. Shiseido was founded by Mr. Arinobu Fukuhara – my grandfather – who started his working life in the dispensary of a navy hospital, but was determined to start his own drugstore, no matter how small. In 1872, he opened his drugstore at the corner of a newly built brick commercial arcade in Ginza, the fashion district of Tokyo, and called it Fukuhara Shiseido. Later, he changed the name to Shinbashi Shiseido, taking the name of the location, before settling on today's name, Shiseido. During the early years, Mr. Arinobu Fukuhara sold European cosmetics, toothpaste, soap and other apothecary goods, and Shiseido evolved into a corner drugstore with a cosmetics department.

As a company founder and entrepreneur, Mr. Arinobu Fukuhara devoted himself to social endeavors such as separating the dispensation and prescription functions in medicine. A visionary, he gave his wife, Toku, the responsibility of managing the Shiseido shop; back in that period in Japanese history, it was very rare for a woman to be given the responsibility of managing a business. Mr. Fukuhara was also very interested in the life insurance business. To study it, he traveled to Europe and the United States. So impressed was he by a visit to the Paris Universal Exposition in 1900 and observations of the business operations of the latest drugstores in the United States that he sent his successor, Mr. Shinzo Fukuhara – my uncle, the eldest brother of the second generation – to pursue a degree from the pharmaceutical department of New York's Columbia University. After Shinzo Fukuhara graduated from the university, Mr. Arinobu Fukuhara made him work as a trainee in a drugstore and cosmetics factory, prior to sending him to Paris for a year – in 1913.

After returning to Japan as a successor, Mr. Shinzo Fukuhara established Shiseido as a limited partnership in 1921 and, subsequently, a joint stock company in 1927. Determined to separate ownership and management, in his role as the first President, he took charge of the prescription of products, design and advertisement, and appointed a close friend from his New York stay, Mr. Noboru Matsumoto, to run the business as Managing Director. As for the family business, Mr. Fukuhara decided his relatives to own real estate. As a result, until today, the family business, though it has not experienced swift growth, has earned constant, stable profits.

Meanwhile, the separation of ownership and management meant that anyone, Fukuhara family member or not, could assume senior management positions in Shiseido. Over the years, this arrangement has not only attracted many high quality personnel but also created an environment in which Shiseido can train them to improve. This culture should perhaps come as no surprise, since education of employees has been a Shiseido tradition ever since it opened its doors as a family business.

In the following years, Shiseido established sales subsidiaries all over Japan, and, after World War II, the company set up more sales subsidiaries, joint venture companies and sales representatives in many countries, starting with the United States, Italy, Hong Kong, and Taiwan. The credit for this progress has to go to the company's policy of developing better human resources by allowing non-family members to become top managers. Among the twelve Presidents in Shiseido's history, only three came from the Fukuhara family, and with an exception of the founder, the other two were promoted to the position only after following the same course as the other non-family Presidents. Today, the Fukuhara family owns only a small portion of its issued share capital, and thus has no dominance in capital ownership. Nevertheless, company Presidents from the Fukuhara family embrace the aura of symbolism that comes with ownership.

As the tenth President of Shiseido, and the third President from the Fukuhara family since its founder, I embarked upon a major corporate reform with the slogan *Starting the Business Afresh*. After retiring from daily business operations, I became an advisor. In my symbolic presence as Honorary Chairman, it has been my role to maintain the social relationships of our company. There may not be a fourth President from the Fukuhara family for some time to come, since no one from the family is currently working for Shiseido. We cannot, however, predict the future.

Even though our founder left no precepts solely to guide *family* members, the following two principles have devolved to each of the succeeding Shiseido Presidents. First, as a private company, we should create a family-like company culture free of politics. Second, we should contribute to the health and beauty of all human beings. Shiseido's cultural capital and corporate atmosphere reflect our fidelity to these principles; the individual traits and aptitudes of each Shiseido manager strengthen this corporate culture, and have become the foundation of our company's growth.

Our founder, and first President, did however, craft Shiseido's five precepts for the corporation *and* the family:

1. **Quality first:** Our prime commitment is to quality.

2. **Co-existence and co-prosperity:** Everyone associated with Shiseido should share its benefits.

3. **Respect for consumers:** Shiseido's priority should be consumer satisfaction.

4. **Corporate stability:** Shiseido should evolve around a firm foundation, with long-range goals.

5. **Sincerity:** Business will always be conducted with loyalty, honesty, and respect.

Throughout the years of our development and growth, cultural capital and intellectual assets have accumulated in the company, and made it possible for Shiseido, both as a company and as a brand, to gain our customer's trust. The founding family's sound philosophy and beliefs begot the Shiseido culture that carried on even after the company's public listing. The product of 129 years of our history, this philosophy and set of beliefs still exists, and I would like to modestly express my hope and my wish that, regardless of whether the Fukuhara name, or family, carries on, the Shiseido Company Ltd. continue making contributions to the world through its long-standing values.

Yoshiharu Fukuhara

Honorary Chairman

Shiseido Company Limited

8

FAMILY DYNASTIES

It is estimated that the average life span of a business is less than fifty years. Family businesses, not known for their longevity, normally survive only one generation, or about thirty years. Nevertheless, a number of businesses have beaten the odds, lasting more than one hundred years, and a few of these have even been around for several centuries. Of these venerable enterprises, a large portion are family-owned. Among the best known examples are Beretta (Italy), founded in 1526; Mitsui (Japan), founded in 1673; or Marie Brizard (France), founded in 1755. Also among this august group of long survivors are the two family businesses at the heart of this chapter: the Takanashi family business was founded in 1661 in Japan, and the Frescobaldi business was founded in 1092 in Italy. Amazingly, they have lasted almost 350 years and more than 900 years respectively.

What unique traits have made the longevity of family dynasties possible? First, they have a ready ability to adapt and change to shifting economic, political and social circumstances. Not only do they survive war and economic recession, they also change considerably over the centuries. They regularly invest in new machinery or new technologies, and they always put top-quality production first. Whenever necessary, the owning families willingly reduce their standard of living during bad years and, traditionally, avoid borrowing money to expand or modernize their businesses. Because they are thus free from repaying loans and coping with crises or difficult economic times at the same time, they are less vulnerable to business failure than many of their competitors.

A majority of long-standing family businesses either own land, and produce wine or trade in spirits or timber, etc. Or they own property, and work as hoteliers, for example. In other words, these eminent family businesses own fixed assets that increase in value over generations. It would seem reasonable to expect that, after ten, twenty or even thirty generations, they would have thousands of members, many of whom might be involved in the business. But this is not the case. Consider the Frescobaldi family. Although they are in the middle of the transition to the thirty-first generation, relatively few family members hold shares, and most of them are involved in the day-to-day business. In general, the main reason for the small number of owners in family dynasties is that, by tradition – although by no means exclusively – these families passed their land and properties on to a single family member in the next generation. By contrast, businesses in other industry sectors often have more family owners, as many as several hundred, but few family members are actually involved in running the business.

The two letters in this chapter reveal another characteristic common to long-running family businesses: the ability to change while remaining close to the original product range. Building on centuries of expertise, long-enduring family companies remain open to market opportunities. They evolve. The Takanashi family started by producing soy sauce, then gradually moved into distribution. Later, the company progressed into distributing beverages, and, most recently, added food distribution and restaurant franchises. The Frescobaldis started as bankers, but they soon became landowners and winemakers. They expanded by acquiring new estates, spread distribution into some sixty countries, inked joint ventures in California, and recently launched their own wine bars.

Lastly, like many other successful old businesses, both of the dynasties represented here respond to new ideas and external advice. They open their company boards and top management positions to talented outsiders. This willingness to hear and consider and to accept and deal with whatever challenges come along is a key trait of dynastic family businesses.

Marchesi dè Frescobaldi S.p.A.

Location: Tuscany, Italy

Turnover (in US$): $ 38.3 million (Dec 2001)

Date of exchange rate: March 31, 2002

Name of local currency: Italian Lire

Number of employees: 181

Activity/industry sector: Winemakers and landowners

Geographic spread of the business: The single largest vineyard holding in Tuscany; partnership in California; distribution in more than 60 countries; new acquisition Friuli (Italy)

Year the business was started: 1092 (1300: year the first wine transaction was dated – 1900: business started grouping of wholly owned estates – 1980: company was founded)

Generation running the business: 30th

Name & position of person writing the letter: Dino Frescobaldi, 30th generation, board of directors

Other family members active in the business: siblings of the author: Vittorio Frescobaldi, chairman and CEO; Fernandino Frescobaldi, vice-president, Leonardo Frescobaldi, vice-president; Maria Luisa Frescobaldi, Benini, director – members of the 31st generation: Bona Marchi Frescobaldi, director; Tiziana Frescobaldi, public relations; Lamberto Frescobaldi, director enolo; Stefano Benini, USA area manager

% of capital owned by the family: 100%

Recipient(s) of the letter: 31st generation members of the Frescobaldi family

Note:
A passion for their land has been passed down from father to son, generation to generation. The underlying philosophy of the Frescobaldi has always been respect for the land – the belief in an unbreakable relationship between the environment, the vine, and the climate.

The Frescobaldi family.

Marchese Dino Frescobaldi to the members of the 31st generation

Dear Successors:

One cannot look to the future and ignore the past. Our family has old roots. It may seem ambitious to say, but the facts are these. In the time of Dante and Boccaccio, the Frescobaldis carried on commerce, above all, banking activities back when the florin, on which the emblem of the Florentine fleur-de-lis was stamped, represented the first coin of Europe. The Frescobaldis loaned money to the king of England and, in return, collected the rights to customs. In Tuscany, they owned land. They had banks and administration offices across our continent: in London, naturally, but also in Bruges, Antwerp, Nantes, Bordeaux and other centres of business. They maintained relations with the Near East. They imported raw materials for their weaving mills. In 1300, one of them, Leonardo, took an expedition to the so-called Holy Land of commercial and military information (with a purpose other than religious devotion). He passed through Egypt and Sinai, and wrote detailed accounts that even today are considered important texts in travel literature.

In Florence, the Frescobaldis had their houses along the left bank of the Arno which, at that time, was the least developed part of the city. In order to connect this area to the centre, one of them, Lamberto, took the initiative to construct one of the first bridges over the river, which was consequently baptized "pons de domo Frescobaldi" (the Santa Trinita bridge now sits there). Like most Florentine families, the Frescobaldis excelled in the arts that made the city great. They also had an important role in political activities. They were part of the class of "magnates," always at the centre of civil strife. Simultaneously, some of them held important posts in the cultural and literary world of the times. Dino, Matteo and Lambertuccio were poets who took part in a literary movement called Dolce Stil Nuovo that changed the view of the Italian language and culture. Today, Dino's verses are included in many school anthologies, but he had, above all, a credit to which the world would be thankful. As Giovanni Boccaccio can attest to, Dino was one of Dante's best friends, and as such, he recovered the first seven cantos of the *Commedia* when our greatest poet was obliged to escape the city quickly for political reasons. Dino saved those cantos and had them brought back to the author and urged him to complete the work. Without this fortunate discovery, the world would probably be deprived of one of Dante's major works.

The story does not end here. When the things of which I have spoken took place, the Frescobaldis were already landowners in Tuscany. In the XVI room of the gallery of the Uffizi, there is a huge geographical fresco (circa 1500) that takes up the entire wall and bears the inscription: *Terre dei Frescobaldi*. The family possessions extended for a long way east of Florence along the Arno, which was an essential waterway for Florentine trade. Consequently, the Frescobaldis could, in practice, have exercised control of the river through which a majority of the economic traffic passed. The Frescobaldis potentially had the future of the republic in their hands.

On their land they cultivated grain, feed, fruit and vegetables, but in particular vines. The wine produced in the Frescobaldis' vineyards already had a large clientele in Florence. Proof of this is the receipts of the purchases made by renowned people, including politicians and famous artists. Because their fortunes were thus rooted to the land, throughout the centuries the Frescobaldis were able to overcome difficult times. As happens in great families, even they knew periods of adverse fortune during the political turmoil that in every epoch marked the destiny of Florence. At various time, some family members had to seek refuge in exile; others were constrained by the same political hazard to change their name. They called themselves among others Montecastelli or Rinieri. But the most difficult moment in the family chronicle coincides with the coming to power of the Medici dynasty. A great hostility began. Together with other traditional Florentine clans, (among them was the Albizzi, one of the most prominent families), the Frescobaldis were staunch adversaries of the new wealthy class. They took part in various conspiracies. After the discovery of one of these conspiracies, one of them, Battista, was sentenced to death.

For political reasons, the banking and industrial activities of the family were penalized. In the time of Lorenzo the Magnificent, Florence reached its maximum splendour. This was the city's golden century. In subsequent centuries, however, the discovery of the new continent brought on a revolution in the world. Trade no longer passed through Florence, and suddenly, the city was no longer the centre of the planet. The nations around the Mediterranean were eclipsed in importance and commercial dynamism by the ones that faced the oceans and great seas. Consequently, Florentine industry decayed. But also at that time a branch of the Frescobaldis, with Giuseppe and Lamberto at the top, tied their name to the production of cloth and brocade. As far as they were concerned, high quality could beat the competition of other countries.

These were the remote origins of the family fortune. With the passage of time, the Frescobaldis continued to be landowners. The value of the land had risen in relation to the primary need to take care of their growing family. During this epoch, the Frescobaldis transformed themselves predominantly from bankers and industrialists into farmers. From their economic and financial power of the previous centuries, they kept the ownership of estates and farms mostly in Val di Pesa and Mugello. Here they introduced innovative techniques and the use of new machinery. They were avant-garde in their use of advanced systems and production. In particular one of them was given the merit for the importation of a seeder from England.

An important event happened in the 19th century that reinforced the economic fate of the family. Leonia, who was the last descendent of the notorious family Albizzi, with whom the Frescobaldis were often tied by the bonds of marriage, in addition to a coming together of destinies, married Angiolo Frescobaldi. Leonia was heir to a great fortune, mostly in the form of land. Angiolo was a conspicuous character for his role in the cover up of the court of the Grand Duke of Lorena. In addition, he had a great passion for and was an expert in art. So this is how the property of the Albizzis, along with the farms of Nipozzano and Pomino, ended up as part of those of the Frescobaldi family.

Ferdinando, the only son of Angiolo, inherited everything. He knew how to maintain the uniqueness of the estate as well as the excellent quality of the products, namely the wine. Ferdinando also had an only son, Lamberto, who, after his father's death in 1940, became owner of a considerable complex of nine farm estates: Nipozzano, Consuma, Poggio a Remole, Montecastello, Castglioni, Montagnana, Corte, Senni, and Valiano.

This is how we have reached our tormented times. The two great world wars of the first half of the last century cut deeply not only into our national society, but also into the life, work relations and the running of the country. At the end of a dramatic course of events, our country, which was almost exclusively agricultural, became a country of mostly industrial transformation. Even the system of sharecropping, which had been ingenuous in innovation for the past century and founded on common participation of the management and earnings of the land by the owner and the worker, had entered into a crisis. Needless to say, the companies of the Frescobaldis had been run for a long time with this system, typical of Tuscany in the time of the Grand-Ducal.

In the world picture, these things came together simultaneously. The economic confines of society continued to open. The systems of autonomy of the single states started to fail, which was also true for agriculture. At that time, the so-called globalisation process took place that with the passing of the years took on a rhythm increasingly more rapid and overwhelming. Some cultivation was no longer economical. Until the last war, the Frescobaldis' farms had produced a bit of everything. But then certain products could be bought in other countries at much lower prices. Consequently, it was necessary to renounce production of goods that were no longer competitive and concentrate on producing those things that were local and of high quality, and thus that could hold a stake in the market.

Needless to say, at this point, the product on which the family business concentrated was wine. With the passing of time, it counted on its prestigious name, which reaffirmed itself over and over again. The wine that came out of the family cantina was already, as we have had the occasion to say, well known in public. It was necessary, nevertheless, to boost not only the production but also the marketing of the Frescobaldi goods to be more in line with the times.

And here is precisely the decisive choice that fell on the shoulders of the last generation of the Frescobaldis, who were willing, despite the circumstances and the difficulties, to hold on to a company they had inherited. This last generation was formed, in the second half of the twentieth century, of the children of Lamberto: five brothers (Dino, Vittorio, Piero, Ferdinando and Leonardo) and two sisters (Maria and Teresa). What was their decision? Rather than divide themselves, they preferred, except in one case, to stay united, giving life to a business structure based on their relationship as a family, to avoid the fate of other important Florentine and Tuscan clans that, in the presence of similar conditions, had undergone an immediate process of division and, subsequently, fragmentation and impoverishment. Despite the fact that the number of the owners of the business had to be reduced for natural reasons—the tragic death of brother Piero and, for personal reasons, the separation agreement of the sister Teresa—the family business thrived.

For his recognizable quality and competence, and by common consensus, Vittorio had to take the reins. All the others gave their contribution according to their respective inclination and attitude. This is how a model case of family business was born. Exemplary it was because particular interests were always subject to calculation and persuasion that was always necessary to take the lead of the common interests of the business. Exemplary it was, again, because the general interest in the growth and in the success of the company confirmed and rewarded the right choices many years over.

The moral legacy for the future generations can be seen from how much and to what extent we have traced the history of the family, albeit only briefly. Recently our family business has had notable success. But nothing could be more wrong than to think that the main and final choices have now been taken and that the problems have been resolved once and for all. Other choices and other decisions await us. The process of transformation of human partnership has not stopped. Rather, it has more likely accelerated. No one is capable of saying what developments will come. For this reason, it is difficult to give advice. We can only hope that the next generation knows to take the best from their predecessors. That means to keep committed to the spirit and to the values that the family has always held to overcome turbulent times. The values are the unity of the members and the branches, however many there will be in the future, the consideration and management of every vision and particular interest, and finally the recognition of the values of the competence inside the family business. This is the letter, this is the message, and this is the patronage for the generations to come.

The old wanderer

Marujin Corporation

Location: Tokyo, Japan

Turnover (in US$): $1.73 billion

Date of exchange rate: average 2000

Name of local currency: Yen (1$US=107.83 Yen)

Number of employees: 2500 (group total)

Activity/industry sector: Holding company: real estate – other businesses: food and beverages wholesaling and distribution, food-related franchises.

Geographic spread of the business: Domestic 99.8%, international 0.2%.

Year the business was started: 1956 (Soya Sauce business: 1661)

Name of the founder and relation to the author: Hyozaemon Takanashi, 28th family master, grand-father of the author.

Generation running the business: 3rd (30th generation of the Takanashi family)

Name & position of person writing the letter: Ichiro Takanashi (Director of Marujin Corporation)

Other family members active in the business: 9 (all males)

Other family members non-active shareholders: 59

% of capital owned by the family: 96%

Recipient(s) of the letter: Next generation, 4th generation in Marujin Corporation (31st generation of the Takanashi family)

Note:
The Takanashi family originated in 1105 (30th generation), the soya sauce business started in 1661(11th generation) and Marujin Corporation in 1956 (3rd generation).

Ichiro Takanashi to the members of the 12th generation

Dear Successors,

Our family, the Takanashi Family, has a long and distinguished history. Our ancestry can be traced back to 1105 in the Heian period to a place called Shinsyu Shinano, the present Nagano prefecture. From generation to generation, family masters have succeeded to the name of Hyouzaemon Takanashi. The present master is the 30th in this line. The roots of the family business, however, go back to 1661 when the 19th family master started a soy sauce brewing business in the city of Noda, in the Chiba prefecture.

Two-hundred and fifty six years later, in 1917, my grandfather, the 28th family master and 9th generation of family business owner, decided to merge our soy sauce business with seven neighboring soy sauce brewers and established the Noda Shoyu Co., Ltd.. this new company later became Kikkoman Co., Ltd, now an internationally famous soy sauce brewer. Although large-scale mergers are a daily occurrence in today's world, in the early 1900s, the seven-company merger was a very rare and drastic measure. Eleven years later, in 1928, with the Takanashis as the major stockholder, a new company called Koami was established to fulfill Kikkoman's wholesale function. In the following generation, the eldest son took over Kikkoman while the younger brother, Nisaburo, took charge of Koami.

Koami's independence later led to the branching-out of the family business. Koami quickly grew as a wholesaler of foods and beverages (after merging with Sanyu Shokuhin last year, it became the fourth ranked company in the industry). One of Koami's initial projects was introducing a Coca-Cola franchise business. This new business, Tokyo Coca-Cola Bottling Co., Ltd. was soon achieving sound market results and, in 1956, became independent as a subsidiary company. Since then, varieties of food and beverage-related businesses have been launched and now form the hub of today's Marujin Group. In fact, today, Marujin Corporation is a joint-stock corporation with a capital of US$ 1.32 billion. This family holding company unifies 17 subsidiary companies and 8 affiliated companies. In the past, we were solely engaged in soy sauce brewing; but as you know, diversification has been our method of business development, and today we continue to launch new projects as the pillars for the next business opportunities.

Family and Business

My grandfather had six male and one female children. Throughout our family history, female members of the family have not been involved in business. But all six brothers shared business responsibilities and took charge of various family business divisions. Out of eleven male cousins in the 30th generation, seven play active management roles in Marujin Group's leading subsidiaries and related companies. Another three chose to take management posts in family businesses that are not under Marujin's umbrella. Along with three non-family directors and three auditors, all eleven cousins, including me, are current directors of the Marujin Corporation, the holding company.

Of course, we face various issues involving cousins' management, but we have been dealing with them relatively well. One reason for our effective dealings is that we grew up watching our parents working together and collaborating. Thanks to our grandfather, who repeatedly taught us the importance of family connections – he liked to say, "brothers and sisters as well as cousins must be kind to each other and support one another" – we have had many occasions for the family gather. These family gatherings have brought us close to each other and built mutual trust. Another reason for our effective dealings with one another is that the very existence of the Marujin Corporation gives us a place where family members can communicate and discuss both business and family issues. Presently, we hold monthly director's meetings in order to share information and discuss a variety of issues. Passing on such management know-how to the next generation is one of our essential missions. As a result, the linkage between family and business remains strong.

The Succession Process

For hundreds of years, succession in the Takanashis' family business followed the traditional hereditary system under which the eldest son became both the family master and the head of the family business. By succeeding to the name of Hyozaemon Takanashi, he inherited the family property. In the absence of a male child, the family had to take in an adopted son to fulfill the succession duty. Following clear precepts of succession, the eldest son or senior persons possessed absolute authority and were expected to display leadership. This well-established succession arrangement, combined with the nature of the soy brewing business, enabled the family to avoid the set-backs of an ever-changing business environment. The Takanashis prospered. But the family's traditional succession arrangement is impossible to preserve in today's society. From the siblings' point of view, the succession system in which the eldest son takes over the entire family property is unacceptable. Moreover, Japanese inheritance tax is one of the highest in the world, and it has become ever more complicated to pass on the family property.

So now, in response to these modern challenges, Kikkoman Corporation has created a unique succession system. Because the company was co-founded by eight neighboring soy sauce brewing families, each family has the right to assume management posts. Under the hereditary system, even after Kikkoman's public stock offering, members of these eight families have continued to assume the presidency. An unwritten law, however, prevents any one family from monopolizing the presidency; the most capable among the eight families are selected. This arrangement, in which representatives of many families compete, enhances the development of capable managers, eliminates the indolence that is said to be typical of family business, and fuels the forces that drive institutional advancement.

Marujin Group, on the other hand, has no definite succession guidelines. Although there is a tendency for the business to be passed on to the founder's son, the size of share holdings often influences the succession process. Nevertheless, we fundamentally believe in selecting a person whose experience and ability suit the Marujin Corporation's further progress. For that reason, we do not hesitate to appoint an outsider if his – or her – qualifications surpass those of our family members. Our ongoing effort to separate ownership and management reflects this approach. At this point, none of you in the next generation is working for the Marujin group, but we are not concerned because we believe that outside experience is a very valuable asset.

The Family Philosophy: Prosperity through Generations

The most important prerequisite for prosperity across generations is clarifying and sharing the family philosophy. Our family philosophy has been handed down since the 17th century in the form of family precepts. These original precepts, I believe, are priceless "live" instructions our predecessors left to us to ensure our success over generations. The following contains a few of these Takanashi family tenets:

1. Parents and children, siblings, couples, and all relatives must be kind and friendly to each other. Take loving care of persons of lower social status. The master must work hard and concentrate on the job.

2. Do not be lazy. Devote yourself to the family business. Know your limits, and do not exceed them.

3. Do not influence others negatively by telling lies or being unreasonable.

4. Do not engage in any sort of gamble.

5. At all times keep the following in mind :

    •   So long as you devote yourself to the family business and do not spend money on yourself, even if you become deprived, everything is going to take care of itself.

    •   A loving, affectionate, and sympathetic person will never become a slave to love affairs.

- Do not ever abandon or look down on people. Save them, and others will not abandon you, and you will have nothing to be concerned about.

The Family Philosophy: Enabling the Next Generation to Succeed

The Takanashi family philosophy has served our family and our businesses well for more than four centuries, and I believe it will probably also be the best guide for your generation. These are the main precepts:

A spirit of family reciprocal relationship

Respect the will and wishes of individual members' while sharing a sense of values in harmony. Be close to each other, and highly value cooperation with and support for one another.

Business vision

Our tradition says, "business is for the good of consumers". We follow this belief, and aim for sustainable progress by investing in projects that are directly linked to or expected to have a beneficial effect on everyday life.

Action philosophy

Avoid any involvement in business activities that go against the good of society.

Social contribution

Do not indulge in personal affairs. Instead, embrace a sense of moral responsibility at all times and contribute to society by every means conceivable.

I have no clear tip or advice on how to carry our business success on through the next generation. What's most important is to keep challenging yourself, and this lesson applies not only to your generation, but to all future generations. Never be satisfied with the status quo, never give up, respect those who support you, and most importantly, never forget to be grateful. These are the principles our predecessors practiced. They should be carried on, and I am counting on you to make them come true.

Ichiro Takanashi

The 30th gen. of the Family

The 11th gen. of the Family Business

Director of Marujin Corp

9

DIFFICULT TIMES

The family letters and the business descriptions in this book might, at first read, give the impression that each of these companies has known only success. But this is far from the truth. Life in family business is not always easy. And not always triumphal. Over 60% of all family businesses never make it to the second generation. So it should come as no surprise that many of the companies in *Sharing Wisdom, Building Values* have been through very rough times. The Strauss family, for instance, has come close to bankruptcy several times. Despite its close calls, Strauss Dairies always pulled through. What ensured their success after years of struggle? Persistence. They simply never gave up. They had faith in their business.

Family businesses, like any other businesses, face failure, economic downturns, competitors, predators, down-sizing and obsolete products, to name but a few of the hazards. To make matters tougher, they have to cope with potential family conflicts and complex succession challenges. The letters from Alberto Falck and Jesus Anaya in this chapter tell a compelling tale of how the two family businesses have confronted market stagnation and succession difficulties. Despite these hurdles, the two families prevailed. How? First, they managed to see the problems, accept them and adapt to change. But even more than seeing, accepting and adapting, they shared two common, and indispensable traits: like the Strauss family, they never ceased to believe in being a family in business. They fought relentlessly for it, even if that meant starting all over again. The two companies that follow are models of determination, for they have succeeded against all odds.

The letters in this chapter carry a message of hope to all family business owners who face the many seemingly insurmountable challenges that, all too often, bring about the demise of family firms. That message is this: among the best prospects for succeeding against the odds are adaptability, honesty, courage and faith.

Falck S.p.A.

Location: Milan, Italy

Turnover (in US$): $600 million (Turnover 2001)

Date of exchange rate: December 20, 2001

Name of local currency: Italian Lire

Number of employees: 960

Activity/industry sector: Electricity and related activities (waste recycling – waste to energy)

Geographic spread of the business: Italy, Turkey, Senegal

Year the business was started: 1906

Name of the founder and relation to the author: Giorgio Enrico Falck, grandfather of the author

Generation running the business: 3rd

Name & position of person writing the letter: Alberto Falck, president

Other family members active in the business: Brother: Ing. Federico Falck (CEO) – cousins: Ing. Carlo Marchi (vice-president) and Dr Ferruccio Marchi (board member)

Other family members non-active shareholders: 15

% of capital owned by the family: 100%

Recipient(s) of the letter: sons of the author, Enrico and Alessandro, students

Note:
The Falck family has been an entreprising family since 1833. The author, Mr Alberto Falck, is the president of the Italian Association of Family Businesses (AidAF).

Alberto Falck to his sons

My dearest sons,

The theme of succession in a family business is a delicate one. It involves a problem that is not only technical and organizational, but one that brings into play many values: historical, sentimental, emotional, interpersonal, and the value of character. Briefly, succession is the meeting point between work and family, between blood ties and patrimonial ties, between the logic of management and the circle of private life, between the sphere of interest and the sphere of affection. So we're on shaky ground – in fact, some fall – but still the succession theme is a crucial one, made even more complex by the additional factor of the personality of whoever will have to take on the role of leader, along with this person's ideas, sensibilities, and abilities, both as head of the company and as a point of reference for the entire family.

Succession is, in and of itself, a traumatic thing: it can cause crises, if for no other reason than the fact that no one is equal to their predecessor. This is true even if the predecessor would like it to be so, perhaps to hand down to his successors not only the position, but himself in person. Also, everyone has his or her own way of being an entrepreneur. One person may act as Executive Officer, the mythical CEO of the Anglo-Saxons, or the PDG of the French. Another might delegate the running of the enterprise, as in our case, to a professional manager, and assume the role of President, which entails taking on the position of a sort of shareholder/manager back-up, so to speak, for the managing director.

Obviously, in the latter case, the rules of corporate governance dictate all the strategic decisions regarding the company, which are therefore the competency of the Board of Directors and/or the Executive Committee. In both of these corporate bodies, the role of President is fundamental.

Actually, I find that this is also the family business organizational model that best keeps pace with the evolution of today's economy and, more importantly, the future. For this model requires a continual supply of new ideas, staying ahead of the competition in the marketplace, and careful attention to risk. In a protected economy, or in a more or less stable one, the "owner" of a traditional company, especially if he is the founder, and also an authoritative and charismatic leader, can guide and run it personally.

Today, running a company requires a plurality of experiences and abilities, including skill in evaluating business situations. Thus, simply holding the title of company owner is no longer enough. Instead, professional qualities of a completely different nature are necessary: the ability to adapt very rapidly to change, to pre-empt it, in fact. The others, the competition, certainly aren't sitting still. And a place on the market, if not taken in time, won't be easy to find..

Therefore, your training must be absolutely in keeping with the times. The next generation will have to be even better prepared than the last. Now, more than ever before, the young people in a family who take charge of a business must receive specialized training: they must be managers. The fact is, we are facing the need to "managerize" entrepreneurial families (if you will allow me this ugly neologism), or at least the members of these families who aspire to a future at the executive level of the company. This does not mean simply being able to speak English well, but knowing how to move on all markets, having a world vision of opportunity, learning to be "in business" in a different way than my generation was or your grandparents were, being able to swim energetically in the strong currents of the global economy and not simply to stay anxiously afloat.

All of this, moreover, doesn't exclude the family as a point of reference. Indeed, the family definitely gives you an added advantage if you consider its patrimonial heritage. The family gathers round the company in moments of crisis, and makes the financial effort to re-capitalize when the need arises. Even in non-crisis times, the family, with its collateral activities in the area, creates an environment that is favourable for the company: often the behaviour of the family is identified with that of the company. This, obviously, obliges the family to behave in a way that is coherent with the actions and the image of the company.

Perhaps all this seems like a golden cage to you, a burden a bit heavy to bear, a sort of collusion among austere moral principles, business demands, and "republican virtues." But you must consider the fact that the business, too, has a decisively positive reflection on the family, because it provides a strong element of association. Two aspects of family – affection and business interests – intertwine. It is clear, then, that the reality of family and the reality of business are integrated, and must be.

On one hand, professional and managerial training, on the other the strong umbilical cord to the family: this, it seems to me, is the synthesis of my "talk" with you so far. Now let's take a closer look at some specific themes.

For you, and clearly for your cousins, too, who are orientated towards the same goal, the first and most important piece of advice I want to give is this: make a *life* choice, *your* choice. Each one of you is certainly free to become a violinist, a doctor, or an antiques dealer, but if you're interested in joining the company, the choice must be made with absolute clarity, so you can prepare yourselves adequately. A life choice means commitment, a desire to learn what you need to learn. If you have no training, you have no competence, and without competence, you'll find yourself coming up against problems that are bigger than you are. Not only that, you'll risk being manipulated by those who are competent. In other words, a life choice imposes conditions; it is what will decide if you are strong or weak, in or out.

Moreover, in choosing to set for yourselves the goal of reaching the executive level of the family business, two primary values clearly come together: love and business interests. That is, the logic of family and the logic of business, the sphere of affection and that of business, the bonds of blood and the natural impulse to be a successful entrepreneur.

The commitment then becomes twofold, involving personality in every one of its aspects, since the family has to perceive the company as a precise intrinsic value, as an inalienable patrimony and unifying element. The person who has made this life choice (and in so doing is delegated the responsibilities of the company by the family) participates in that principle and, at the same time, the imperative of business as such. From this comes the condition of working not only for oneself, but for the entire family, to guarantee the family the continuity and expansion of that value.

All this translates into the added advantage I mentioned before.

One thing to keep in mind is that, at least in a company like the one that carries our name, you won't simply be "heirs" called upon to take over, with honour, the patrimony left you by the founder, or actually by the "re-founders": each generation re-founds the company, on the basis of what has been handed down, but also renewing it to adapt to the times, or even changing it completely.

Without going too far afield, Falck was created by its mythical founder (your great grandfather) in the steel industry. Then, after the war, the second generation reconstructed it and developed it to the point where it became one of the great Italian industries. Yet my generation had to accept the fact that business was stagnating and, then, that the steel business had run dry.

A re-foundation followed, involving a dramatic and radical reconstruction, with a similarly dramatic and radical laceration in the family. Today, our core business is electricity, the production of which has stimulated, in turn, other activities – first in the energy sector with co-generation, and then with activities related to energy in some way, such as waste to energy, or waste recycling solutions for the environment.

Steel is still around, but only for a few specific processes. In substance, Falck today is something different from what your great grandfather created and what your grandfather and great uncles recreated. Falck has been transformed in its nature and its structure. Just consider that fact that thirty years ago there were 16,000 people in the company, and now there are just over 800 of us.

This is what we, of the third generation, have had to do. And you? What will you do? Considering how things are going, it's likely that you'll continue on the same path and grow even more, because energy has a great future, just as the environmental sector does. But you, too, will have to re-found the company in some way – and that will be your entrepreneurial legitimisation. You'll close some activities and open new ones, select strategies, react to a different world-economic context. You'll move ahead, innovating and developing, because this is what an entrepreneur has to do, and this is what you have to prepare yourselves to do.

I still need to add a couple of comments regarding aspects of personality.

For example, character. In the long run, character is what counts, because it is the basis for strength in making choices, courage in making decisions, and resoluteness in taking risks. Character is often considered an immutable point of departure, a natural gift like the colour of one's skin or the length of one's nose. But this is not so. Nature gives us a tendency [toward one type of behaviour or another], but we can correct it, train it, mould it. What I mean to say is that you need to "take care of" your character. In more practical terms, if you tend toward impetuosity, you must learn to contain aggressive behaviour, or if you are too compliant, you must demand submission. If you make this life choice, you also have to engage in character building, so you won't one day be thrown off balance by your own behaviour.

Another fundamental point is tenacity: not stolid stubbornness, but lucid determination, often necessarily garnished with patience. If you take a path that you truly believe is the right one, you mustn't let any difficulties get you down, from complications, bureaucracy, or any other "wrench in the works," because in the end you'll succeed. It's difficult to create a complex project, devoting intelligence and resources, to then see your project blocked for months or even years for lack of a rubber stamp, or because of some quibble, or the "provisions" of some abstruse interrelated regulation. And yet with tenacity you'll attain your goal, believe me.

Train yourselves in this, too. Prepare yourselves psychologically to resist and persist, especially since you're working in a "rubberstamp-obsessed" country like ours.

Finally, I'd like to comment on the theme of communication. As soon as you announce your intentions to become entrepreneurs, you will automatically be inundated with requests (valid ones, too) to create the company's financial mechanisms, managerial techniques, organizational models, office circular systems, methods of analysis and any number of other things directly connected to the business. Absolutely right, but I think it is no less essential to talk about communication, which is at the same time both the nervous system and circulatory system: the good health, even the life of the organization/business, depends on communication, just as the corpus of the family/business does.

Our market image is nourished by correct and fluid – and above all systematic – communication in two directions. First, toward the source of nourishment, so to speak; that is, toward the world of finance. (For our capital-intensive enterprise this is essential, even existential. Today one works primarily with ideas, not only with one's own capital and, in so doing, utilizes project financing assured by a banking system and a financial market.) Second, toward the society at large, because working in the sectors of energy and waste means depending to a great extent on the assent of others, public powers as well as individual citizens. These are the stakeholders to take into consideration. Therefore we need to make ourselves known; we need to give a foundation for the trust we ask; we need to be credible.

The family/business relationship is nourished, too, by communication: How can the culture of "the company as an intrinsic value at its core" take root and mature if little or nothing of the company is known, except by those few family members who run it?

All family members need to be aware of the strategic choices the company makes and the motivation behind them, the value of stock as the right to true participation, the major problems and possible solutions, because all this is a condition basic to unity. What's more, this allows a correct and unanimous reaction in critical moments, lacerating turning points. As you know, we have meetings at least twice a year specifically for this purpose.

There is a second objective, no less important, which is to stimulate interest in the souls of the younger generation. Communication toward the family is necessary, therefore, also to lay the groundwork for an orientation which, one day, may become a life choice. The first step in this process is the training that the family is committed to giving the new generation.

At this point I'm a little embarrassed. I'm sure I've said important things, clear and pragmatic for me, as I'm the one who has lived them and still does, but I'm afraid you'll take them as rhetorical. You may believe me out of personal admiration, but you lack the experience that can anchor my points to the ground for you. Don't throw them in the bin, though. Simply put them in your pocket, then pack your bags and go to work for a few years in another country. On your own. When you come back, we'll take them out and talk about them again.

I have total faith in you.

Papi

Translated and re-printed from an Italian book entitled *"Lettere al futuro – Il passaggio dell'azienda da una generation all'altra. Le testimonianze di 33 imprenditori di successo"* (Gianfilippo Cuneo, Milano: Baldini&Castoldi s.r.l., 1999). Used with permission of the author of the letter and the publisher.

TYLSA GROUP
(Anaya Kessler family group)

Location: Torreon, Coahuila, Mexico

Turnover (in US$): $38 million

Date of exchange rate: April 2, 2002

Name of local currency: Mexican Peso

Number of employees: 637

Activity/industry sector: Metal mechanics (steel pipes for oil, agriculture, industry); electric power distribution towers; components for electrical installations; commercial outlets for construction supplies.

Geographic spread of the business: Manufacturing in Torreon, Sales in Mexico, Latin America and USA.

Year the business was started: 1945

Name of the founder and relation to the author: Mr. Zelman Kessler.

Generation running the business: 2nd

Name & position of person writing the letter: Jesus Anaya, Chairman of the Board, founder's son in law.

Other family members active in the business: Eduardo Anaya Kessler, founder's grandson.

Other family members non-active shareholders: Elena Kessler de Anaya (wife), Liliana Anaya Kessler (daughter) and Concepcion Chavez de Kessler (founder's widow).

% of capital owned by the family: 100%

Recipient(s) of the letter: The above-mentioned.

Note:
Torreon City is a commercial zone where industry is scarce. Grupo TYLSA was a pioneer in metal mechanical production activities in the region.

Background of TYLSA Group

Zelman Kessler arrived in Mexico during World War II. At the time, the Torreon zone was the largest cotton-producing area in Mexico. Cotton bales need metallic ties, so Mr. Kessler started manufacturing them.

Later, Mr. Kessler married Concepcion Chavez, and they had a daughter, Elena Kessler.

Soon thereafter, the company started up commercial outlets for construction supplies.

Mr. Anaya married Elena Kessler in 1970.

In 1973, Jesus Anaya, an engineer by education, started two companies dedicated to manufacturing and installing building structures, tanks, electrical sub stations, etc.

In 1976, Mr. Kessler bought a mill for steel pipe manufacturing. From time to time Mr. Anaya helped, adding new installations and implementing operational improvements to the mill. It was a difficult time for Mr. Anaya, working in an unstructured environment with unclear direction for the business. This situation prevailed until 1980, when Mr. Anaya took over the operations of TYLSA.

When Mr. Kessler passed away in 1988, Mr. Anaya's companies merged with Grupo TYLSA. Today the Anaya Kessler family owns all the shares in the combined business.

In 1995, Mr. Eduardo Anaya, the son of Jesus, went into the business after graduating from industrial engineering school. Eduardo is now in charge of new ventures and main projects.

Liliana Anaya, Jesus' daughter, is a textile designer, and does not work in the family business. All family members have seats on the board, including Mrs. Kessler and Elena Anaya.

The whole TYLSA Group now has 10 companies, including production, services and commercial companies. It is preparing for the succession to the next generation.

April 10, 2002

Jesus Anaya to his wife and children

March 2000

BUILDING OUR FUTURE TOGETHER

After all the memories we have recently shared on the backgrounds of our families, we should now – more than ever – make a serious effort to think about our future as a business family. To make our expectations come true we should clearly define them. By so doing, we may be able to outline the family vision as a *common* dream, and we may thus be able to avoid our weaknesses and build on our strengths, and therefore not repeat our failures and mistakes.

To give life to the family project, we must find all the factors that can unite us in harmony, respect, love and understanding. To establish common goals and courses of action, we must leave behind individual secrecy and isolation as we define the problems we now face as a family. This is a vital process: it may be tough and painful. To build our future together, all family members have to take part; we will need to share our individual opinions and visions.

As I understand the lessons we have learned from other families, our own family will stand a better chance of improving, progressing and reaching its goals if it can formulate clear, common goals, and follow a process of change that involves all its members. Each of us must be thoroughly convinced that our family project is, right now, our most significant concern.

We must therefore attend all family meetings with a positive and unselfish attitude, and without imposing our personal points of view. Our participation must be honest. We must always look for the best way to express our opinions without jeopardizing the harmony among us. Through this exercise, we can communicate clearly what we think and feel, without urging – or demanding – the others to change.

We owe each other, whether elders or youngsters, respect as human beings, each with his or her own personality and way of being. Respect depends not solely on age, but on our willingness to grant others the chance to be their own selves: we must not try to push them to fit our personal models of a wife, son, sister or relative. Respect starts inside ourselves. It begins with trying not to think wrongly of others, not correcting them, pointing out their faults or using harsh words against them. We must take care of what we say, both with words and with our body language.

Communication starts before a couple gets married, during courtship. It changes through time, involving children and other family members. It develops over the years, positively or negatively. Unfortunately, however, communication sometimes decays, and then dies. At other times, such as this one, communication is greatly desired for the sake of harmony.

Harmonious communication must be an internal need arising from two individuals who wish to say something to each other. Both must choose the best moment, adopt the right attitude and listen. They must also await the proper moment to communicate, taking care that harmony persists throughout their conversation.

Love is undoubtedly the foundation for the family. It is the essence of family interrelations, the indispensable element for comprehending and interacting satisfactorily with all family members. It keeps us together. Love helps us regard the great problems that exist in all families around the world – no family has ever been exempt – merely as bad moments that will soon pass.

In our family, we regard our past as a wonderful time full of good experiences and sad mistakes; yet, we foresee our future with great hopes for improvement. We want to prepare ourselves well to build a better future together. And it is love that keeps us here. This love is sometimes very hard to express, but family ties will always translate into a commitment to help each other. Whether with a hug or a kiss, or with a simple, kind word, very deep inside, our hearts always yearn to show affection for our loved ones.

We must make an extraordinary effort to get to know each other intimately. Our familiarity may help us better understand each other, especially our reactions. To achieve common purposes, self-knowledge and a positive attitude are vital. In our process of building a better business family, with all these ingredients, we may be able to find the opportunities we seek for the future. We must cast aside all our past mistakes and failures and search, united, for the values and principles that lead to a future full of happiness.

You realize, of course, that until now I have not mentioned the business. It is more important for me to have a functional, loving, harmonious family. The kind of family I wish for is essential for appreciating, protecting and enhancing the moral and economic legacy the previous generation passed down to us, which gave us the opportunity to respond satisfactorily to the younger and future members of the family.

Your loving husband and father,

Jesus

Jesus Anaya

Chairman

TYLSA GROUP

10

SOCIAL RESPONSIBILITY

"Prosperity, if not rooted in a solid morality, will provide the seeds of its own destruction."

Sage – Order of the Knights of Malta – 16th century

Events and newsworthy matters in recent history – the Rio Summit on the preservation of the environment, the use of child labor by household-name companies, the rise of groups protesting against globalization, the events of September 11, 2001 in the USA, and the downfall of Enron leading to tens of thousands of job cuts – have led to debate about the ethics and social responsibility of firms across the world. How socially responsible should a firm be? Some groups, led by well-known economists, argue that the single purpose of a business is to generate profits and increase shareholder value; businesses, they believe, should not be involved in philanthropy. Others claim that social responsibility is one of a firm's main paths to long-term sustainability.

No doubt businesses need to make profits, but recent surveys show that they cannot ignore the correlation between social responsibility and business growth. More than ever, consumers are aware of the moral stance of companies. According to MORI Ltd, a survey firm in London, "In four years (1998-2001), the proportion of consumers saying that a company's social responsibility is very important to them when purchasing a product or service has increased from 28% to 46% of British adults." Studies of investor behavior indicate that investors react favorably to socially-responsible firms: they buy their stock and increase their financial value.[7]

But what does social responsibility mean to family businesses? Family

businesses have business reasons or family reasons – or both – for being socially responsible. They have typically lived in a given community for a long time.
They care about their environment and are well-known local figures. They
often give a lot of time and resources to their communities although they usually try to keep their involvement as quiet as possible. Business families often
want their children and grandchildren to work in the business and therefore,
may have a greater natural incentive than non-owner managers to improve
their firm's environment. Consider: Paulig was an early investor in environ-
mentally-friendly production processes. Maus was among the first companies
to introduce re-cycling processes in its home country. Miele decided against
moving out of its community to seek cheap production locations. Developing
Brazil is at the center of Algar's value charter. Some families also use community work to share an activity, to give the younger generations an opportunity
to experience team-work and leadership from an early age, to promote harmony among family members and to pass on their values.

As the three testimonies in this chapter illustrate, in terms of social
responsibility, several other characteristics of family businesses distinguish
them from non-family businesses. The three – S.C. Johnson (USA), the Mulliez
family office (France) and the Murugappa group (India) – are extremely successful businesses that have enjoyed steady profits and growth over the years,
but they are also families and businesses with a heart. However, their efforts to
be socially responsible take different forms. S.C. Johnson meets its responsibilities through the business. It leads numerous programs to develop environ-
mentally-friendly products and production processes. Family members in the
business take time from their jobs to do community work, setting the example
for their employees and encouraging them to get involved in similar activities.
For Murugappa and Mulliez, community work is done either by family members who are not active in the business or by "business active" family members
in their spare time. The business provides the necessary financial resources –
funds or dividends – but time spent is a "private" family matter.

Socially-involved family businesses are not new. The three business
families in this chapter follow guidelines and precepts established long ago:
Sam Johnson's father and grandfather were very active in their community;
André Mulliez's grandfather and father were religious people who cared about
developing their region economically; and the founder of the Murugappa
group established a basis for the family to support education and health, the
two pillars of the third and fourth generations' community work. These families do much more than give money. They set an example by working personally and keenly for good causes. And they work to transmit their strong social
values to the next generation from a very early age.

[7]Jones, R. & Marrell A. J. (2002) Signaling Positive Corporate Social Performance.
Chicago: *Business and Society*, 40(1), 59-78.

SC Johnson & Son, Inc.

Location: Racine, WI, USA

Turnover (in US$): $4.5 billion (SC Johnson)

Number of employees: 9,500

Activity/industry sector: consumer products (famous brands include: Shout, Windex, Mr Muscle, Ziploc, Edge, Glade, Brite, Raid, Pledge, Pronto, OFF, Scrubbing Bubbles, etc.)

Geographic spread of the business: operates in nearly 70 countries and products are available in over 100 countries

Year the business was started: 1886

Name of the founder and relation to the author: Samuel Curtis Johnson, great-grandfather

Generation running the business: 4th and 5th

Name & position of person writing: Samuel C. Johnson, 4th generation, Chairman, Johnson Financial Group and Chairman Emeritus S.C. Johnson & Son, Inc.

Other family members active in the business: Dr. H. Fisk Johnson, S. Curtis Johnson, Helen Johnson-Leipold, Winnie Johnson-Marquart

% of capital owned by the family: 100%

Note:
The Johnson family of enterprises is comprised of: SC Johnson, a $4.5 billion global consumer products company; Johnson-Diversey, a $2 billion dollar global institutional products company; Johnson Outdoors Inc., a $500 million global recreational products company; and, Johnson Financial Group, a global financial services and banking business with more than $2 billion in assets.

Samuel C. Johnson, Chairman Emeritus

From left to right - H. Fisk Johnson, Gene Johnson, Sam Johnson, Winnie Johnson Marquart, Helen Johnson-Leipold, S. Curtis Johnson.

Samuel C. Johnson

There is more volunteer activity in the United States than in almost any other place in the world. It is estimated that 89% of US households contribute to charitable causes, and more than four out of ten Americans regularly perform volunteer service with an estimated value at around $70 billion in donated time. According to the most recent INDEPENDENT SECTOR'S Giving and Volunteering in the United States, American volunteers log in an average of 24 hours per month each. In nearly every city and town in the United States, the United Way serves as the focal point of volunteer agencies and activity.

My grandfather was one of the founders of the united community fund in Racine, Wisconsin (USA). The fund brought volunteer agencies together to more effectively raise money for their purposes. But raising money is only part of voluntarism. Even more important is the good portion of free time volunteers devote, at no pay, to charitable organizations. As the population ages, more people than ever before will be available and willing to volunteer. In Racine, many retired people work hard as volunteers sometimes giving more time than they ever could have when they were employed.

People can get excited about volunteering. It has a two-way benefit – a benefit to the community or organization and a benefit to the volunteers and their companies. My father believed that we could only have a healthy environment inside our company if we had a healthy environment in the community outside. We wouldn't be able to hire good people for the company, for example, unless we had a good community for them to live in. If business owners would just volunteer, in constructive ways, to improve the ten blocks around their places of business, we might well cure a good portion of our urban blight.

A family-owned business, because of its roots and flexibility, or a locally owned business, because of its self-interest, has a much greater sense of community responsibility than a company with headquarters in a distant city. But still, for voluntarism to really take hold in a company's culture, a key executive must set the example by being involved personally. I spend about two days out of every seven on what I call "not-for-profit" activities.

For Johnson, the heart of voluntarism is *people* serving their communities – teaching, counseling, advocating legislation, serving on agency boards. My grandfather, a church-going man, believed in corporate philanthropy. He believed that, by various methods, the corporation should give something back to the broader group of consumers from which it has earned its profits. Providing jobs, he believed, was important, but not enough. Following my grandfather's footsteps, my father always encouraged our people to involve themselves in social, cultural, and educational projects that enhanced the qual-

The Great Workroom at SC Johnson. The original idea for the Great Workroom was, in part, a result of the beliefs of both architect Frank Lloyd Wright and Herbert F. Johnson, Jr. (then president of the SC Johnson). They believed that employees needed direct access to each other in order to promote efficiency and a greater sense of cooperation. SC Johnson believes that the fundamental vitality and strength of its organization lies within its people, and its employment policies and practices reflect the value we place on the contribution of all employees. The Great Workroom utilizes almost one half acre of workable floor area. Today, there are three major departments in the room: Finance, Accounting, and the Law Department. Since 1939, the Wright-designed "center of creativity" has illustrated SC Johnson's fundamental belief that only the best people working in the best environment can create the best products. (Courtesy of SC Johnson)

ity of life. Today, an SC Johnson employee in the U.S. is giving an average of about 100 hours to a local charitable organization. In the U.K., the company closes its doors one day a year and 500 employees spread out through the local community performing projects and providing services that fill local needs.

It was either my father or my grandfather who started giving five percent of the company's pretax profits to charity. My father passed the heritage of voluntarism on to me, and I am grateful for it. Now, the corporate philanthropic policies of SC Johnson are not fundamentally different from those of the Johnson family.

At SC Johnson, in fact at each company in the Johnson family of enterprises,[8] corporate social responsibility means "corporate opportunity," not doing only what is expected morally or required by law, but rather, applying our corporate and personal talents and resources to make a significant difference in our communities. We recognize that the health of our communities, our schools, and our governments bears on the health of the corporation.

How do we meet our social responsibilities? First, corporate employees are involved in community activities. We encourage and facilitate employee involvement. Second, Johnson employees are involved in government and legislative action, not only legislation that directly affects the company, but also on the legislative needs of our communities and neighbors. Third, we contribute cash. Since World War II, there has been a precept in the corporate world that if you want to be seen as part of the responsible community, you should be contributing approximately one percent of your income. In cities like Minneapolis and Chicago, you also hear a lot about the "Two Percent Club." SC Johnson has been a member of the rare "Five Percent Club." In giving, we are not alone: today, corporate donations to U.S. non-profit organizations amount to $11 billion.

There is – and probably always will be – a running debate about the merits of corporate philanthropy. There are those who oppose almost all corporate charity. Nobel-winning economist Milton Friedman is purported to be the headmaster of the give-nothing school. He has said, "This is a fundamentally subversive doctrine; the claim that business should contribute to the support of charitable activities is an inappropriate use of corporate funds in a free enterprise society." But even Friedman makes exceptions. First, he says that closely held corporations may contribute directly to charity "to lessen the tax bite." He also approves of contributing to local institutions, such as hospitals, colleges, museums and parks when they provide marginal returns to the company. Our philosophy at Johnson is hardly so self-centered.

I'd like to challenge the criticisms of corporate contributions. Most corpora-

tions conduct their social responsibility programs on an enlightened self-interest basis. If your headquarters is located in a broken-down neighborhood, for
example, you may find it hard to hire good employees. Shouldn't your company improve the neighborhood so you can hire better people who will, in turn,
improve your profits? Isn't it appropriate for corporations to support the uni-
versities they recruit from? Such help, after all, better assures the quality of
their future managers. And isn't it also appropriate to support university
research in an area that might have some technological importance to the corporation in the long run?

Our company heavily supports The Johnson Foundation, which my father
founded. The Foundation's main role today is to convene conferences related
to sustainable development – including education, the human environment,
and social equity. Conferees gather at Wingspread, my father's home and the
place I grew up, which has been converted into a conference center and
Foundation headquarters. I feel privileged to serve as Chairman of an
esteemed board of trustees who are dedicated to making Wingspread a place
for decision makers and active people to meet and discuss the most important
problems our global society is facing. Perhaps out of these conferences will
come solutions that make a difference.

Samuel C. Johnson

Extracts from *"The Essence of A Family Enterprise. Doing Business the Johnson
Way."*© Samuel C. Johnson, Chairman, Johnson Financial Group and
Chairman Emeritus. S.C. Johnson & Son, Inc.

Used with permission of SC Johnson & Son, Inc.

[8]The Johnson family of enterprises is comprised of SC Johnson, a $4.5 billion global con-
sumer products company; Johnson-Diversey, a $2 billion dollar global institutional
products company; Johnson Outdoors Inc., a $500 million global recreational products
company; and Johnson Financial Group, a global financial services and banking business with more than $2 billion in assets.

Murugappa Group

Location: Chennai - India

Turnover (in US$): $850 million

Date of exchange rate: 23/11/01 (1 US $ = Rs. 48.08)

Name of local currency: Indian Rupees

Number of employees: 22,500

Activity/industry sector: Manufacturing and distribution of Abrasives, Steel Tubes, Bicycles, Chains, Fertilisers, Sugar, Tea, Confectionery and Sanitary ware. Financial Services.

Geographic spread of the business: Mainly India – very small presence in UK & USA

Year the business was started: 1898

Name of the founder and relation to the author: The Late Dewan Bahadur Arunachalam Murugappa Murugappa Chettiar - Grandfather

Generation running the business: Third and Fourth

Name & position of person writing the letter: Mr. M. V. Subbiah – Director External Relations and Innovations

Other family members active in the business: M/s M. A. Alagappan, A. Vellayan, M. M. Murugappan, M. M. Venkatachalam, A. Venkatachalam, Arun Murugappan and Arun Alagappan

Other family members non-active shareholders: M/s M. V. Murugappan and S. Vellayan

% of capital owned by the family: Between 35% to 75%

Recipient(s) of the letter: 4th Generation: A. Venkatachalam, Arun Murugappan, Arun Alagappan and S. Vellayan. 5th Generation: Arun Vellayan, Nana Vellayan, Muthu Murugappan, Veeru Murugappan, Muthu Venkatachalam, Subbu Venkatachalam and Arun Venkatachalam

Note: The list of quoted companies is as follows: E. I. D. Parry (India) Ltd., Coromandel Fertilisers Ltd., Tube Investments of India Ltd., Carborundum Universal Ltd., Cholamandalam Investment & Finance Company Ltd., Parrys Confectionery Ltd., Parry Agro Industries Ltd.

Shri. AMM. Murugappa Chettiar (extreme right) with his father Dewan Bahadur AM. Murugappa Chettiar and mother Mrs. Valliammai Aachi.

MV with the Murugappa family

M.V. Subbiah to his grandchildren on the history and values of the family business

My dear grandchildren and members of the 5th generation of our family,

Knowledge and culture in India used to be transmitted from generation to generation through an oral tradition. It was assumed that fathers would tell their children everything about history. When I grew up, there never was any difference between siblings and cousins. We ate together, went to school together, and went on holiday together. Be it at the breakfast table, family lunches or Sunday get-togethers…we were subtly trained to believe in collective wisdom. As these events included members of every generation, each was an investment in the future, with an air of informality and an atmosphere of trust and mutual respect. But in the past 30 to 40 years, life has changed a lot. We miss out on our fun and games and camaraderie.

Nowadays, you live far apart, and we take little time to share our family tales and history with you. I have decided to write a few notes so you will learn how our family business became the diversified business it is today and also so that you will become aware of the key values that serve as the glue of our family and the fuel of our business success. Over the years, the institution of the family has nurtured me with great values and provided me the space to hone my skills. Building a business organization, having family experiences and growing my understanding have taught me to invest time in keeping the family together – the combined efforts of people will always be greater than just individual skill.

I was blessed to be born in the family of Murugappa. Our business history all started with a visionary man – my grandfather – who went to Burma at the age of 14 as a clerk to work with another business family from close to our village. Being a very smart young man, in three years, he picked up the business of indigenous banking: money lending and trading. His employers were very happy and soon gave him a lot of responsibility. At the end of the third year he came back and got married.

In 1894, he put together his own money and the dowry he had received from his wife and started his own banking and trading business in Burma. His first son, my eldest uncle Murugappa, was born in 1902, exactly a hundred years ago. All together, he had five daughters and three sons. Each of the three sons – my father and my two uncles – joined him in the business. From the very outset, grandfather lived by the principles of the Arthashastra. One was, "The fundamental principle of economic activity is that no man you transact with will lose; then you shall not." He had a vision of building his own empire and at the same time building the institution of the family.

In those days, the British ruled India, Burma, Malaysia and Sri Lanka (Ceylon at the time). My grandfather saw a business opportunity: the British banks opened only for certain hours, but grandfather and other community members did most of their trading and banking outside those hours. People needed to place their money when British banks were closed, so here was a tremendous opportunity. With his three sons, grandfather expanded, opening a branch in Burma, and then in Malaysia and Sri Lanka. An agent in each branch looked after his business, and grandfather gave each agent a 25% share in the business, what we in modern terms would call stock options. For the early 1900s, this was very far-sighted.

My grandfather trained his successors in an interesting way: we were all sent to one of the agents for training. (I was the last to be trained his way.) Banking and trading was just a one-man, one-room show, sometimes with a couple of clerks. You basically lived with the agent, first serving as an office boy for the agent's errands, like buying cigarettes and going to the post office for the mail. After 3 or 4 months, if the agent thought you did that well, he made you sit with the cashier and start writing the cashbook. Later, if you managed these added tasks well, he allowed you to buy or sell a little in the trade. In 1952, when I finished my school finals, my eldest uncle Murugappa did the same: he sent me for training to an agent in Sri Lanka (Ceylon), which at that time was the only overseas office that was still trading. I can never forget my first day as a "Podian" – a peon. I, the son of the owner, was asked by the agent of the family to go and buy paan for him. Not knowing the language, and in a strange country, where was I to go? Curiosity and inquisitiveness – these are great qualities for continuous learning and they have stood me in good stead ever since. This experience also taught me humility and to respect the dignity of labour. If I didn't tally the cash book every evening and put the cash box into the safe (he had one key, I had the other), I was not to have dinner! This was how discipline was drummed into every successor.

Our family has strong values and beliefs, most of which emanate from my grandparents, and most of which guide the way we do business. Our first business value is 'Adhere to ethical norms in all dealings with shareholders, employees, customers, financial institutions and the government'. In India, businessmen were seen during the 15 to 20 years after independence as crooks. Nobody believed a businessman! We had to say, 'We are different and our reputation is more important than making money'. We have not grown as fast as some of the other families that started when we did, but our reputation with the government, financial institutions, customers and employees is excellent.

Our second business value is 'Provide value for money to customers through quality products and services'. The third is 'Treat our people with respect and concern, and provide opportunities to learn, contribute and advise, recognise and reward initiative, intuitiveness and creativity'. This goes with our fourth value, 'Maintain an organisational climate conducive to trust, open communication and team spirit'. Over the years, we have done more work on values in the business than in the family itself. We realise now that we have taken the family for granted. In future, we shall devote more attention to communication, and building team spirit and trust in the family. Our fifth business value is 'Maintain the kind of operations that befit our size, but reflect moderation and humility'. We do not seek publicity. We keep a low profile, which is unique in our part of the world. Our next value, the sixth, is about preserving the environment: in each of our businesses, be it plantations or chemical plants, we do our utmost to preserve the environment.

Our seventh value is that we give one per cent of the profits of all the companies to our family foundation, which runs four schools, four hospitals and a small research centre that villagers can access free of charge. This value, and our corresponding role in the community comes from my grandfather, too. He was inspired by a couplet in a 2,000-year old Indian book: "If you build a house and dig a well the water is available only for your family/But if you build a water tower, the whole community can share that water." Grandfather built his house in 1917, he built his water tower in 1920 and he built the first hospital in 1924.

He told us, "Concentrate on two areas of community work, education and health, and never give it free." To go to school they have to pay a fee, to go to a hospital for treatment they also have to pay, even if only one rupee (one fiftieth of a dollar). Thereafter the doctor's treatment and everything but medication is free. Grandfather used to say, "Give charity for free, and people will never respect it. If they pay, they will feel they have earned it. They've got to get value for their hard-earned money'. Community work also gives our ladies a key role: they run our foundation. They spend time in the schools and the hospitals, ensuring not only correct housekeeping and maintenance, but also strategies, expansions, relationships between parents and teachers, and children and teachers, and among hospital patients, doctors, nurses, and all other relationships.

Our eighth and last business value is about change: 'Grow in an accelerated manner by continuous organisation renewal, consistent with the values and the beliefs'. We have always believed strongly that if we don't renew ourselves continuously, if we don't create change ourselves, change will overtake us and we will be in trouble.

From the early days of my grandfather, over a hundred years ago, and throughout our history, we have been able to foresee the economic history of India. This foresight has helped us evolve and keep changing the business we are in. When independence came, we saw an opportunity to manufacture goods in India, and we were among the first to join hands with British and Americans as part-ners to start manufacturing products in India. So, we are no longer in banking and trading; we are in industry. We are in manufacturing and distribution of abrasives, steel tubes, bicycles, chains, fertilisers, sugar, tea, confectionery and sanitary ware. We are also in the financial services like leasing and hire pur-chase. Nowadays, we realise we must move away from manufacturing because as a country, we are no longer the most competitive players. We are, therefore, examining our strengths and starting to build our next businesses, all the time keeping in mind that we are Indians and that whatever we do, we must first do it in the best interests of the country and then in the interests of the family. We are considering a move into information technology (IT) and services. The question is: How do we move into IT from the manufacturing business we started in 1947. And how quickly can we build expertise?

Besides business values which are by the way, held by the family for genera-tions, we have a number of unwritten rules from Indian tradition introduced by my grandfather. These rules have been updated from time to time. The whole family accepts and respects these rules because they work well for our family. They govern how we work together, our compensation, the way own-ership is passed on from one generation to the next, and who can work for the business. Besides his three sons, my grandfather employed one of his sons-in-law, which did not work. My uncle later tried again in his generation, and again it did not work. The culture and training of the sons-in-law, who came from different business families, were very different from ours. They struggled to adjust to our values. In my generation, we tried again, hiring one of my brothers-in-law, but again it was unsuccessful. So we decided only sons and sons' sons would work in the business.

Members of our family do not work in seclusion. Non-family managers are given the highest management and board functions. In India, most of our com-panies are public, limited companies, but we also apply the same rule to our private company, which is right now becoming our holding company. Generally, our policy is to have a maximum of two family members on the board of any public limited companies. The others are independent profes-sionals from outside the family. We own a minimum of 35% and a maximum of 75% of the public limited companies.

The board of the private company ensures that the family strategy reflects the changes that are taking place in the world, particularly in India. For young family members joining the business, we are looking at new business opportu-nities, and we are also making decisions about what businesses to exit.

We have been very fortunate in our family because, with only a five to seven year gap between generations, we have no generation gap and we do not know the generation-gap problems so common to other families. The oldest and youngest of various generations have also worked together for over 30 years. My uncle and my brother always worked very much like two brothers, consulting one another on all business decisions. If there is a communication problem, we always go to the person who has good contacts or good communications with one other family member for a talk. He advises us, and we act accordingly. We network amongst ourselves and use our differences as strengths. Almost every five years, someone enters the business, which makes it easy to transmit values, experience and wisdom.

My grandfather took an unusual view of business ownership. Seeing with his own father that the British-imported primogeniture system did not work for us, he said, 'I have already lost a son. At the age of 65 I don't want to work anymore. I'm going to divide the property while I am alive. I remember what happened with my father and don't want to do that'. So he divided his wealth into three equal shares and said, 'This is a shareholding, but you must be united'. In subsequent generations, we have applied the same rules. The shares are always distributed one third per family branch, starting from my grandfather's three sons. My eldest uncle had only one son who received 33% of all ownership. My father had three sons, so I only became an 11% shareholder and my two brothers alike. The youngest uncle had two sons who each received 16.5%. We have inequality among the individual shareholders, but equality among the three family branches.

So, each of the three family branches has divided its wealth equally among the male members of the next generation, and all have retired from the business at 65. We are one of the very few families to have a retirement policy and fortunately we don't have to face situations where 90 year-old men want to interfere with day-to-day operations.

With time, we will probably have quite a large number of young people entering the business. We are encouraging all of you to study to the age of about 23 or 25, to do at least a university degree and then get some exposure to other businesses before entering ours. We feel it is fundamental that the family maintains both ownership and executive roles in the business.

Ownership, however, does not mean that the ones who have more shares play a bigger role in the business. We feel that all capable men should work in the business. We are much better off than most of the people in the country, and therefore, our job is to develop the country, not just worry about our own wealth. To make sure that all members of the family can maintain a similar standard of living, all members of the same generation working in the business get the same salary. What differs though, are our bonus levels, which depend on how well the particular business we run is performing.

Apart from the values and the rules and ownership policies I have outlined above, I would like to share with you my profound learning from the elders.

One day in 1963, after two years of working as a shop superintendent in the cycle factory, my eldest uncle Murugappa asked me how things were going in the factory. As a good, loyal family member I told him how bad and useless the expatriate boss, the general works manager, was and that I, who had been trained in the U.K., could run it much better. He listened patiently and said good things that encouraged me. As I was leaving he asked whether I maintained a record of my views. My affirmative reply caused him to seek to read them. He then said that when I became the boss, I could run the plant the way I wanted to, but as long as I was a superintendent, I had no right to be critical, as I was there to learn and had to respect the boss. From my position as shop superintendent, I could not see the 'whole'. I saw only one side or part of the story. He told me not to be critical, but rather to try to be logical and convince the boss, even if it was his fault. My diary had to be shredded. This incident taught me an invaluable lesson in integrity and discipline.

My eldest brother, M.V. as he was popularly known, was a great scholar in Tamil. From him I learnt my lessons on delegation. He, too, was moved by the Thirukurral. I quote a passage from the Thirukurral in which Saint Thiruvalluvar writes about employee empowerment in Kural 517. In translation, it reads: 'After having considered this man can accomplish this by these means, let the leader leave with him the discharge of that duty'.

It is often said that five fingers are not alike, but that it takes all of them together to grasp or accomplish things. Our family recognized this early. My brother M.V. understood each and every person and delegated matters according to the person's strengths. He always had a smile and never lost his temper. My other brother, Muthiah, was shrewd in finance and a clever negotiator. He believed in transparency during negotiations. Under him, I learnt the art of negotiating both with JV partners and with trade unions, all of which stood me in good stead while I went to EID Parry to transform it and with later assignments.

Upon reaching 65 years of age, M.V. passed the mantle of business leadership to me. Normally, leadership should have gone to my immediately older brother Murugappan, who should have succeeded MV. However, brother Murugappan wished to pursue his interests in technology, ecology and environmental preservation. His magnanimity in asking me to take on the leadership role has no parallel amongst Indian business families. He continues to play an active and important role as head of the family.

So you can see that I have been a very fortunate person right through my life. My family always provided opportunities for me to grow both individually and affiliatively. When I took over as head of the business 6 years ago, all I had to do was keep the momentum going with the help of excellent people within the organisation, all of whom have the values the family stands for. Over three years, my older brother Murugappan, my cousin Alagappan, nephews, Vellayan, Murugu and Venky and I dialogued under the facilitation of Dr. Ashok Ganguly about the transformation required within the family and the business, and their governance as we entered the millennium. We created a supervisory board with three non-executive directors, Mr. N. S. Raghavan, Dr. Marti Subrahmanyam and Mr. Natalino Duo, and also our CFO Mr. Partho Datta, all of who are not family members. We benefit immensely from their counsel and advice. A few months down the road, we had no problem in requesting that Mr. Raghavan take over as Chairman of the Supervisory Board.

Moving from family to board and on to building the Murugappa Institution was thus a one-hundred-year saga spanning three generations. We are lucky the fourth has also been groomed in the same environment and is taking on the mantle to move the institution from 'ownership to trusteeship'. This was adequately reflected in a speech by my nephew Murugu in Rome in October 2001. He said, 'We consider ourselves custodians to a heritage and trustees to a tradition, both built on togetherness, trust, mutual respect, ethical values and above all dignity, independence and discipline. As the scope and magnitude of the family and business leadership changes, we are preparing ourselves for the great challenges ahead'.

I would like to conclude by stressing three things we have done that are dear to our family and key for our future success. The first is family cohesiveness: throughout our history, our unity has been our strength. I remember the day my uncle called me (I was the black sheep of the family) and gave me a wooden pencil and asked me to break it. I took it and snapped it easily. Then he gave me six pencils together and said, 'Now break them'. I couldn't. He said, 'I hope you have learned your lesson'. I had. Our strength lies in being together and maintaining the family's reputation. The second key to our success is maintaining and transmitting our values. The third key is that: we should all play our role as good Indian citizens and help build the country.

You are our future and our pride and I have full confidence that you will keep the Murugappa family flag flying high wherever you are.

Subbu

Mulliez Family Office

Location: Roubaix, North of France

Turnover (in US$): $21,358 million (Auchan financial report 2000)

Date of exchange rate: May 8, 2002

Name of local currency: Euros

Number of employees: over 150,000

Activity/industry sector: retail (Auchan, Décathlon, Pimkie, Kiabi, Leroy-Merlin, Flunch, Saint-Maclou, etc.)

Geographic spread of the business: entire world

Year the business was started: 1915

Name of the founder and relation to the author: Louis Mulliez Lestienne (1877-1952), grandfather

Generation running the business: 3rd and 4th

Name & position of person interviewed: André Mulliez, 3rd generation, honorary and founding president of "Réseau Entreprendre"

% of capital owned by the family: family 85%; employees 15%

Note: The company has 475 family associates. All family members above 25, including in-laws, are shareholders.

Interview with André Mulliez

In September 2001, André Mulliez received the "Légion d'honneur" in Paris, France. He did not receive it because he belongs to one of the most entrepreneurial families in France or because of his tireless contribution to the family business association over 50 years. He received it because of something unique he brought life to in 1986: Nord Entreprendre (North Entrepreneuring) and its related organization, Réseau Entreprendre (Entrepreneuring Network). Since its creation, Réseau Entrependre has been behind the founding of 870 businesses that have created 6,600 new jobs in France.

To understand how such an amazing contribution to society came to fruition, have a quick look at where it all started: the Mulliez family. André Mulliez's grandfather, Louis Mulliez Lestienne (1877-1952), started a little textile company in 1902 in Roubaix, in the north of France. He had 11 children, most of whom were born entrepreneurs: each of the brothers developed businesses related to the textile industry. In 1952, the brothers met with some of their older nephews and, under the motto "all in all" (together in each of the businesses), they decided to develop their businesses within a family association. Each family member aged 25 would have the right to become an associate and purchase shares made of a portion of each of the businesses. To guarantee the commitment of all family members, this agreement is renewed every 10 years. Today, the family counts 850 members, of which some 475 are family associates. In a striking example of family unity, all descendants of Louis Mulliez, whether male or female, age 25 or older – and their spouses – are family associates. The family, mainly in retail, owns companies such as Auchan, Décathlon, Pimkie, Kiabi, Leroy-Merlin, Flunch and Saint-Maclou. Together, these companies employ more than 150,000 people around the world.

André Mulliez' father, Louis Mulliez Cavrois (1901-1974), was the first-born son of the second generation. He was hard-working, receptive to the emerging syndication movement, open to the world. He was also a devout Christian. Louis and his wife, Pauline, had 13 children, of whom André was the fifth. Louis taught a number of values to his children. He taught them not to be frivolous with money and invest it well. As far as the family wealth was concerned, he always said, 'A man's dignity is in establishing his standard of living with his hands. Do not use your wealth for anything else than buying a house for yourself and your family and investing in your business'. He taught his children to be hard-working and efficient. He educated them not to judge people, but to try to understand them, and to be involved in the community.

These values are still central to André Mulliez, 72. Although he keeps a low profile, takes the tram like any other citizen, and has a very small, simple office, his door is always open for people. He works with people and listens to them. André Mulliez entered the family business in 1952 after graduating in management at the Lille Business School. Like all Mulliez family members, he started at the bottom in the family business, a requirement still today for family members who want to join. No Mulliez enters the business unless he/she has the necessary qualities for it, and all start at the bottom. Until 1958, André Mulliez managed very small businesses in the group. His uncles, realizing that he was competent in finance, tax and accounting, asked him to take care of the family office's legal and financial affairs.

He eventually became vice-president legal and finance for the whole family office. From 1976 to 1986 he returned to one of the family owned companies, the well-known Phildar, a retail business that sold high quality knitting yarn. As of 1986 he was back as vice-president legal and finance at the family office level. Following his father's precepts all his life, André Mulliez had two types of activities: the family business and his personal voluntary involvement in the community. He gave a lot of time administrating schools, the local Family Allowance Office, and a regional bank. Today he still presides over the destiny of three newspapers he saved from bankruptcy, a spiritual centre, Réseau Entreprendre, and Chemins d'humanité (Pathways to Humanity), an association he created to provide management training to young priests. Since 2001 he has also been the president of the French committee for the evaluation of support to very small businesses.

Together with his wife, Françoise, a warm-hearted woman with small laughing blue eyes and a strong sense of family, they had seven children and 25 grandchildren. Speaking about them, André Mulliez says, 'I always tell my children and grandchildren that they should build their lives on three pillars: emotional life, professional life and social life. I tell them – mainly the young ones – "be careful, life can take back any of the three unexpectedly! If the two other pillars are well-balanced, you will get back on your feet. You can lose your emotional life, but if you have a good job and friends around you, you will make it. You can lose your job, and with the help of your wife and friends you will make it. You might have to move, lose your surroundings and your friends, but if you do it with your family and for a good job, you will make it." I give this point special emphasis for those between 25 and 35 who are passionate about their professional lives to the point that they tend to forget to invest precious time in their emotional and social lives, be it friends or community involvement. I tell them, "Beware. Look around you. Life is full of examples of people who made that mistake and are unhappy."'

André Mulliez' involvement in society has taken many forms, all based on his abiding belief in the value of understanding people and helping them. He says,

'In the last years I worked at Phildar (1976-1986) the situation gradually deteriorated. Life was changing and women rapidly lost the habit of knitting. Production dropped from 12,000 to 2,000 tons of wool. We had no other choice than to lay off 600 employees. It made me physically ill. I could not stand it. My family was used to creating jobs, not losing employees. I spoke to twelve members of my family who were as distressed as I was to see so many jobs go, and we agreed: "We have to lose these jobs. There is no other way, but we shall make amends by creating employers who, in turn, will generate employment." We invested our time and money and started Nord Entreprendre in 1986 the same way we would have started any other business.

'Here's how we operate: an entrepreneur comes to us with a new business project. We evaluate the candidacy, and if we believe he/she has a chance of success, we finance the project and support the entrepreneur. What do we mean by support? For each entrepreneur we find an experienced entrepreneur to be a mentor for three years. Mentors meet at least once a month with the entrepreneurs and are not compensated for their involvement. They do it because it is fun to be part of a new venture and also because they learn so much from the young entrepreneurs. We finance the projects by providing a loan between 15,000 and 45,000 Euros, free of interest and without guarantee, for a maximum of 5 years. Should the entrepreneurs succeed, they have a moral obligation not to pay back to the association, but to help other new entrepreneurs.

'We do not support all types of businesses. Eighty percent of all new businesses created in France employ one person only. We do not support any of these businesses. What we want is to be behind businesses that will generate employment. We give preference to the 4% of all new businesses that will generate between 3 and 10 jobs. In 2001 there were 8,000 such businesses in France, and we supported 205. We received a total of 2,850 requests, studied 855, presented 269 to our boards and accepted 205. The companies we support are from all kinds of business sectors, from production to distribution to services in all kinds of industries.

'Emulating the Nord Entreprendre model, we gradually opened new associations in different parts of France and grouped them under the name Réseau Entreprendre (Entrepreneuring Network). Today we have 21 associations, 1,400 members, 2,500 business-leader mentors and 870 winners. On average we have a continuity rate of 86% after three years (national average: 62%) and 74% after five years (national average: 50%), which indicates that we have an efficient concept. A survey of our winners indicates that, after 7 years, on average they employ 17 people. Extrapolating from this figure, today we have with all the companies we have supported a potential of approximately 11,000 new jobs

– 6,600 have already been created and the rest will be created in the coming years.

'A large number of businesses, family businesses and regional banks support our efforts. We are beginning to obtain recognition at the national level and are looking into how to encourage this concept to take root in different countries in Europe, Canada and Latin America. The thing that annoys me most is that if you look at statistics, you realize that out of the 25.5 million workers in France, 14 million work in private businesses. Publicly quoted companies employ only 3.5 million people. Sixty percent of the 14 million who work in private businesses work in companies that employ fewer than 50 people. That leaves 8.4 millions workers in private companies that no one speaks about. Journalists, radio stations, television channels and even members of government speak only about listed companies - the rest are widely ignored.'

Réseau Entreprendre is by no means André Mulliez' only social organization: Chemins d'humanité (Pathways to Humanity), another of his initiatives, trains priests in management. 'When I had to make 600 employees redundant at Phildar, like any good Christian, I was severely criticised when I went to mass. I said to myself, "You have two options: either you stop going to church – they are all stupid anyway – or train them." In August 1996 I got inspired and filled 16 pages of paper on how to train priests. Wondering whether I should keep these papers or destroy them, I gathered a few friends and asked them what they thought about my ideas. To my surprise, they said, "There is definitely something in it. Train priests in management? That's interesting and new, let's ask a few bishops." The bishops we presented the concept to were interested, so we prepared a program. The first year, fifteen young priests joined us, the second year fourteen, and so on.

'The program is far from easy: over a period of two years it is six weeks full-time from Monday at 9.00 am to Friday 5.00 pm, and if they do not commit fully to the program it doesn't work. What amazes me after six sessions is to see the level of commitment of these young priests. To me this is the best proof of the quality of our program. The second interesting result is to see the friendship that develops among them. Their target for the first week is, in groups of four or five, to create an imaginary business. They quickly discover that capitalists are not necessarily bad people, that they help finance business, an idea that is new to them. In the second week they approach the development of businesses using human talents and management tools. The third week looks at illnesses and remedies. It criticises all aspects of a business. The next weeks consist of a summer job, discussing the changes in the world and the management of a country. They end on a three-day total immersion in a company. The whole program is based on testimonies: business people come in to share their experience rather than give a lecture. It is a wonderful program and it works.'

André Mulliez has a lot to say about transmitting values in the family, mainly around social responsibility. 'My father did it with me. He showed me that caring about money was not a purpose to have in life. Money is a means to reach your goals. He was open to the world and always committed to voluntary work. He encouraged us to do the same. At the age of 19 I was working at the renovation of our town. We worked hard but it brought a great sense of pride and belonging.

'What I try to do with the next generations is to talk to them. I spend a lot of time with them, my own children included, and of course for them the best sermon is action and example. Nord Entreprendre is a good illustration: of the 12 cousins who grouped to start it we were all between 35 and 55 years old, i.e. of the 3rd and the 4th generation. Working together on a common project is a great way to transmit values. I also tell the next generations that they should not be too judgmental of others. People most often do something stupid because they have been hurt in some way. We should try to reach out to them and discover why they hurt. If you can ascertain that, you can start to understand them.'

The Mulliez family is also involved in charity and other social work outside the business. According to André Mulliez, 'One key thing you have to understand about our family: we do not mix business and family goals. The businesses are there to be businesses, grow and generate employment and results. In turn, the family members receive dividends and can invest them as they wish. Individuals are free to contribute as they wish to whatever projects they want. Some years ago a few family members created significant funds. Today about 30 family members are involved. The funds – each independent from the others – provide support every year to a total of 200 associations of our choice worldwide, most of them in France and Africa. Further, Isabelle, Chantal and Christophe, members of the 4th generation, along with Luc, Jeannette and Raphaëlle from the 3rd generation, have recently created Le Maillon (The Link), an association that provides support to charities on the one hand, helping them formulate and present their projects, and to the donors on the other hand, helping them in their consideration of requests for assistance and in the decision-making process. In any case, before giving, as we do in all other aspects of our lives, we ask that a few rules be respected: we ask for a profit and loss account from the past years, we ask for a balance sheet, we want to know the people in the associations, we want to know how they will spend the money, and we verify that it was done accordingly.'

'In a few words, I would summarize by saying how proud I am of my family,
of the values we share and of the unity we have.'

André Mulliez

CONCLUSION: LESSONS LEARNED

Reading through the letters, it is interesting to see the marked differences among the families and businesses behind them. In size, the businesses range from small, with approximately 100 employees, to very large, with seven companies having between 10,000 and 150,000 employees. In turnover, these businesses range from US$ 12 million to over US$ 20 billion. These figures may not be representative of the family business world, where the vast majority of businesses are small- to medium-sized; nonetheless, examples and ideas from the families that took part in this book can serve as inspiration for family businesses of all sizes.

The businesses represented in these letters come from every industry sector: primary (winemaking, agriculture, landowning); secondary (production of metal parts, ballpoint pens, consumer products, appliances, food, dairy products, pharmaceutical products, cosmetics, publishing and toys); and tertiary (distribution and dealership, retail, banking, education and telecommunications). They also embody great cultural diversity, with letters from fourteen countries and a number of religious backgrounds. The generation of the family running the business ranges from first to thirty-first generation, with a majority in the third or fourth generation. The number of family owners ranges from 1 to 475; family ownership varies from 1% to 100%, with five listed companies, although a large majority have over 90% family ownership. The number of family members involved in managing the business ranges from one to twenty-three.

When we started work on this book, we were looking for this diversity. To give a broad idea of what life in a family business can be, we sought learn-

143

ings from businesses and families that were as different as possible. However, regardless of the diversity among these families and businesses the number of similarities is striking. This concluding chapter explores the similarities in terms of business, family, ownership and new developments.

Similarities in the Business

The first striking similarity is the number of businesses that were created by strong **visionary leaders** (BIC, Murugappa, Al Khonaini). These leaders were ahead of their time in their strategy, or in the manner in which they handed over the leadership and ownership of the business. Often they were pioneers in their own fields. Not only creative and successful in their time, these leaders also managed to transfer their passion and commitment to the next generations, who perpetuate the founder's dream with passion (Radio Flyer) and/or are market leaders in their products, structures, or processes (Miele, Paulig, Chupa Chups, SC Johnson).

A number of the families in this book also have managed to keep alive a **strong entrepreneurial** spirit. Many of them can boast a series of successful entrepreneurs in the past, which is very inspiring for the present generations. Among others, Miele recently received a marketing award in Germany, Kenny Yap of Qian Hu was elected best entrepreneur of his region, and Ardath Rodale was chosen best international woman entrepreneur.

Another similarity is in how these families keep a **long-term perspective** while maintaining a **strategic freshness** by having a remarkable ability to change and adapt (Paulig, Algar, Lombard Odier Darier Hentsch, Murugappa). Families like the Frescobaldis, although they are in their thirty-first generation, have gone through tremendous changes and growth over the last decade alone. Other families show a stronger commitment to their own instincts than to the generally accepted market wisdom. Miele, for instance, opted for product focus when most competitors were diversifying; although their size and results would have made them an ideal floatation candidate, they decided to remain private; they decided against the market trends of down-sizing and relocation and thereby gained employee loyalty. The Takanashi family in Japan entered strategic alliances long before alliances became common. Each of these families has moved in directions that were right for them, even if it went against prevailing management theory or knowledge.

In most cases in *Sharing Wisdom, Building Values*, the family members who are working in the business are highly competent managers. They are professionals with **strong business skills** and expertise (De Agostini, Lombard Odier Darier Hentsch), and they usually make no compromise on quality (Miele, Strauss, Radio Flyer, Shiseido). They treat their family business like a business, with a perspective of growth and maximizing long-term value. They commit only to excellence and are ready to take difficult decisions (Rodale, Paulig, Strauss) such as cutting divisions, selling part of the business and letting go of control in order to bring in expertise, if and when it is necessary for the business.

In addition to these management skills, family members working in the business are often business people with a heart, **ethics** to match, and commitment to a wider cause. For a number of them, the growth of the business is tied to what they feel is their duty towards their community or their country (Mulliez, Algar, SC Johnson, Murugappa). They have dedication to and love for their business (Miele), and for them, the real value of the business is in its intangible assets: values, culture and human talent. This is why remaining private is important to them. Ardath Rodale expressed it beautifully, "We are a company with a soul."

These families also treat their **employees** (family and non-family), their shareholders, their clients and their distributors with great respect. Family members usually enjoy working together, and they welcome competent non-family members to their boards and the highest levels of management (Shiseido, Maus, Frescobaldi, Henkel). Also, they usually trust, develop and empower their employees. A number of them have even been elected to the ranks of the best companies to work for in their respective countries (Algar, Rodale, Johnson).

Similarities can also be observed in the **succession process**. Most families have strong rules (written or not) about succession, but if need be, remain flexible and adapt quickly to the circumstances. They privilege long-term planning and take time to transmit the management of the business, board positions and ownership. The higher the number of generations – the larger the number of family members – the more time and care they take to stake out common ground and find common values and a **common vision**. It is also interesting to note that, in effect, in companies like Maus, Murugappa, BIC, Henkel and Miele, the outgoing and the incoming generations work together over a significant number of years (between ten and forty) to ensure that expertise and values are well transmitted.

Similarities in the Family

A significant number of families in this book have achieved long-term **continuity of the family** in the business: twelve families are making the transition to the fourth or ensuing generation. This is quite exceptional. In the field of family business, it is usually estimated that no more than 4% or 5% of all family businesses survive as independent businesses beyond the third generation.

Strong values are usually transferred from the founder of the business to the subsequent generations. Families are the keepers of values and rules, and they make sure these values and rules are transmitted at an early age. Dr. Zinkann from Miele said that he already knew in his childhood that he would share the leadership of the business; he grew up knowing and accepting this fact. The Takanashis in Japan have had the same family charter for generations. Their key principles are based on respect, humility and generosity. In most of the cases (Mulliez, Murugappa, Paksoy, SC Johnson) we witnessed a sincere identification by family members with their family values. In these families (Al Khonaini, Strauss) deep love and togetherness are the sources of success, and help resolve conflicts and arguments. Similarities are also apparent in the trust family members have for one another, in the way they stick together in difficult times (Anaya, Strauss, Falck), in the way they find **strength** in their unity (Murugappa, Follett, Miele), and in the way they build on their differences and their different skills.

Most families are also highly involved in their communities. Through voluntary work and **social engagement**, they contribute to making their environment and the world a better place.

Above all, we witnessed a great sense of **pride** that these families have in their business and accomplishments, in their family and in their family name.

Similarities in Ownership Issues

It is striking to see that, even in large to very large family businesses, a significant amount of equity is kept in the family. Even in cases such as BIC, a listed company, Marcel Bich made sure, before the company was floated, that the family would have sufficient voting rights to retain control over key strategic decisions.

The Maus and the Murugappa cases provide interesting, successful examples of unequal individual ownership where family members are given equal opportunities, roles and responsibilities in the business.

New Developments

Although formal **succession processes** and **governance structures** were virtually non-existent in the past, most of these families have realized – or are realizing – that they have been fortunate in the past in that their predecessors intuitively took the right paths. Today, these families are formalizing their processes. They are putting in place rules and structures that give them good control over what is transmitted to the next generations, and how it is transmitted. They have also implemented – or are implementing – clear separations among business, family and ownership issues.

The **role of the family** and of family values is attracting more emphasis (Murugappa, SC Johnson) and families are choosing successors or teams of successors who are not only highly competent business people, but who also are strong defenders of the family values (Maus).

We are also witnessing a new, enhanced role of ownership (Mulliez, Paulig). Evermore, family shareholders are trained to be **responsible owners.** Family shareholders are well aware of their rights and duties, and the ones who are not working in the business are regularly informed about the evolution of the business. Gaining ground is also the concept of **stewardship** of capital (Follett), where family members find that it is their responsibility to grow and nurture the asset they have received in order to transmit it to the next generation. This concept of stewardship was beautifully expressed by a participant at a conference who said:

"A family business is not a business you inherit from your parents. It is a business you borrow from your children."

BIBLIOGRAPHY

Aronoff C.E., Astrachan J.H., & Ward J.L. (1998). *Developing Family Business Policies: Your Guide to the Future.* Marietta, Georgia: Family Enterprise Publishers.

Aronoff C.E., & Ward J.L. (2001). *Family Business Ownership: How to be an Effective Shareholder.* Marietta, Georgia: Family Enterprise Publishers.

Aronoff, C.E., & Ward J.L. (1996). *Family Business Governance: Maximizing Family and Business Potential.* Marietta, Georgia: Family Enterprise Publishers.

Aronoff C.E., & Ward J.L. (1996 reprinted from Nation's Business, April 1992). The critical value of stewardship. *Family Business Source Book II.* Marietta, Georgia: Family Enterprise Publishers, 711-712.

Aronoff C.E., & Ward J. L (1992). *Family Business Succession: The Final Test of Greatness.* Marietta, Georgia: Family Enterprise Publishers.

Aronoff C.E., & Ward J. L (1992). *Another Kind of Hero: Preparing Successors for Leadership.* Marietta, Georgia: Family Enterprise Publishers.

Aronoff C.E., & Ward J. L (1992). *Family Meetings: How to Build a Stronger Family and a Stronger Business.* Marietta, Georgia: Family Enterprise Publishers.

Barnes L. B., & Hershon S. A. (1976). Transferring power in the family business. *Harvard Business Review, 54*(4), 105-114.

Beckhard R., & Dyer G. W. (1983). Managing continuity in the family-owned business. *Organizational Dynamics, 12,* 5-12.

Bich L. (2001). *Le Baron Bich – Un Homme de Pointe.* Jerusalem, France: Editions Perrin.

Cuneo G., & Preti P.P. (1999). *Lettere al futuro – Il passsaggio dell'azienda da una generazione all'altra. Le testimonianze di 33 imprenditori di successo.* Italy: Baldini&Castoldi.

Danco L.A., & Ward J.L. (1996 reprinted from FBR, 1990 3(4)). Beyond Success: The Continuing Contribution of the Family Foundation. *Family Business Source Book II.* Marietta, Georgia: Family Enterprise Publishers, 576-581.

Danco L. A., & Jonovic D. J. (1987). *Outside Directors in the Family Owned Business.* Cleveland, Ohio: The University Press.

Danco L A. (1982). *Beyond Survival: A Business Owner's Guide For Success.* Cleveland, Ohio: The University Press.

Danco L. A. (1980). *Inside the Family Business.* Cleveland, Ohio: The University Press.

de Visscher F. M., Aronoff C.E., & Ward J. L (1995). *Financing Transitions: Managing Capital and Liquidity in the Family Business.* Marietta, Georgia: Family Enterprise Publishers.

Dyer G. W. Jr. (1996 reprinted from FBR 1988, 1(1)). Culture and continuity in family firms. *Family Business Source Book II.* Marietta, Georgia: Family Enterprise Publishers, 212-221.

Gallo M. A., Corbetta G., Dyer G. Jr., Cappuyins K., Montemerlo D., & Tomaselli S. (2001). Success as a function of love, trust and freedom in family business. Monographic 4, IESE, International Business School, Spain.

Gallo M. A. (1997). Delaying the succession in family business. *FBN Newsletter, 17,* 3-4.

Gallo M. A. (1995). The role of family business and its distinctive characteristic behavior in industrial activity. *Family Business Review, 8*(2), 83-91.

Gersick K. E., Davis J. A., McCollom Hampton M., & Lansberg I. (1997). *Generation to Generation: Life Cycles of the Family Business.* Boston: Harvard Business School Press.

Hämäläinen M., & Arnold J. (2001). *125 Years of Enjoyable Moments – Paulig.* Helsinki, Finland. Paulig Ltd.

Jones R., & Murrell A.J. (2001). Signaling Positive Corporate Social Performance. Chicago: *Business and Society, 40*(1), 59-78.

Kenyon-Rouvinez D. (1997). Boards in family businesses: What the owners say about their structure and value. FBN Annual World Conference, The Netherlands. *FBN Proceedings*, 130-150.

Kets de Vries M. (1996). *Family Business - Human Dilemmas in the Family Firm.* London, England: International Thomson Business Press.

Korman M. D., & Hubler T. M (1988). Odd Couples in the Family-Owned Business. *Family Business Source Book I*, Family Enterprise Publishers, Marietta, Georgia, 512-517.

Lansberg I. (1999). *Succeeding Generations: Realizing the Dream of Families in Business.* Boston: Harvard Business School Press.

Lansberg I. (1996 reprinted from FBR 1988, 1(2), 119-143). The Succession Conspiracy. *Family Business Source Book II*, Business Owner Resources, Marietta, Georgia, 70-86 (including 3 –circle model p.72).

Lansberg I. (1995). Succession as a structural change: What happens when siblings and cousins take charge? FBN World Annual Conference, El Escorial, Spain. *FBN Proceedings*, 3-15.

Levi S. Y. (1998). *Strausse – The Story of a Family and of an Industry.* Jerusalem, Israel: Keter Publishing House.

May P., Sieger G., & Rieder G. (1999). *Familienunternehmen heute – Jahrbuch 2000.* Bonn, Germany: Intes Akademie für Familienunternehmen.

Neubauer F., & Lank A. G. (1998). *The Family Business: Its Governance for Sustainability.* London, England: Macmillan.

Ogunsulire M. (2001). A letter to the Younger Generation. *FBN Newsletter, 30*, 18-20.

Peterfriend S., & Hauser B. (2001). *Mommy are we rich? Talking to children about family money.* Rochester, MN: Mesatop Press.

Poza E. (1996 reprinted from FBR 1988, 1(4)). Managerial practices that support entrepreneurship and continued growth. *Family Business Source Book II.* Marietta, Georgia: Family Enterprise Publishers, 290-303.

Sonnenfeld J. A., & Spence P. L. (1989). The parting patriarch of a family firm. *Family Business Review, 2*(4), 355-375.

Sonnenfeld, J. A. (1988). *The heroes farewell – what happens when the CEO retire.* New York: Oxford University Press.

Tagiuri R., & Davis J. A. (1992). On the goals of successful family companies. *Family Business Review, 5*(1), 43-62.

Ward J.L. (1994). Is strategy different for the family-owned business? *Family Business Review, 7*(2), 159-174.

Ward J.L. (1991). *Creating Effective Boards for Private Enterprises: Meeting the Challenges of Continuity and Competition.* San Francisco: Jossey-Bass.

Ward J.L. (1987). *Keeping the Family Business Healthy: How to Plan for Continuing Growth, Profitability, and Family Leadership.* San Francisco: Jossey-Bass.

Whiteside M. F., Aronoff C.E., & Ward J. L (1993). *How Families Work Together.* Marietta, Georgia: Family Enterprise Publishers.

Williams R. O. (1992). *Preparing Your Family To Manage Wealth.* Marina, California: Monterey Pacific Institute.

(2002). *Corporate Social Responsibility – The WBCSD's Journey.* Geneva, Switzerland: World Business Council for Sustainable Development.

(1996 reprinted from *The Family Business Advisor*, 1994). So That Your Values Live On: Ethical Wills. *Family Business Source Book II.* Marietta, Georgia: Family Enterprise Publishers, 704.